Classroom Practice Exercises to accompany Perrine's Literature:
Structure, Sound, and Sense

Thomas R. Arp
Southern Methodist University

Greg Johnson
Kennesaw State University

Prepared by

Carole Hamilton
Cary Academy, Cary, NC

Robert H. Rempe
Bishop McDevitt High School, Harrisburg, PA

For the Advanced Placement Program*

WADSWORTH
CENGAGE Learning·

Australia • Brazil • Japan • Korea • Mexico • Singapore • Spain • United Kingdom • United States

*AP and Advanced Placement Program are registered trademarks of the College Entrance Examination Board, which was not involved in the production of, and does not endorse, this product.

WADSWORTH
CENGAGE Learning

ISBN-13: 978-1-439-08287-4
ISBN-10: 1-439-08287-1

Wadsworth
20 Channel Center Street
Boston, MA 02210
USA

Cengage Learning is a leading provider of customized learning solutions with office locations around the globe, including Singapore, the United Kingdom, Australia, Mexico, Brazil, and Japan. Locate your local office at: **www.cengage.com/global**

Cengage Learning products are represented in Canada by Nelson Education, Ltd.

To learn more about Wadsworth, visit
www.cengage.com/wadsworth

Purchase any of our products at your local college store or at our preferred online store
www.ichapters.com

Credits appear on pages 215–216.

Printed in the United States of America
1 2 3 4 5   14 13 12 11 10
ED166

Contents

PREFACE

Preparing for the AP English Literature and Composition Examination takes a lot of work, but it is well worth the effort. First and foremost, it offers the sheer pleasure that comes of reading fine literature. In addition, it helps students develop their ability for discerning, thoughtful analysis and solid, persuasive writing. These are gifts and skills that last a lifetime. In AP, it really is the case that it is the journey, not the destination, that matters.

Still, the AP exam can seem daunting to both students and their teachers. It is our hope that *Classroom Practice Exercises* will help allay anxiety about it. Gathering in one place thirty-eight literary selections with a total of five hundred multiple-choice questions, ten essay prompts, and two complete practice tests, this book provides concentrated exercises for efficiently and effectively preparing for the test.

We appreciate the valuable assistance we had in writing the book. We want to thank Vinetta Bell and Sandra Daye, for their thoughtful comments on our writing and the presentation of ideas, and Margot Mabie, for wrestling the many pieces of this project into a finished book.

Carole Hamilton
Robert Rempe
July 2009

ABOUT THE AUTHORS

CAROLE HAMILTON has taught English in grades 7–12 for fifteen years. A member of the faculty at Cary Academy, in Cary, North Carolina, she has taught both AP English Literature and Composition and AP English Language and Composition. Expert in critical analysis and rhetoric, she also coaches the debate team, and she has contributed articles on literary analysis to several publications. She has been an AP reader since 2007.

ROBERT REMPE has been teaching English for forty-seven years, most of them at Bishop McDevitt High School in Harrisburg, Pennsylvania. With a doctoral degree in English, he has taught on both the high school and college level, in this country and abroad, and he writes extensively on Shakespeare, his specialty. He has been a reader for the AP English Literature and Composition Examination since 2004.

INTRODUCTION

Not long after the start of the school year, you begin to have a sense of how your students will do come May, when they take the AP English Literature and Composition Examination. Some will do very well. They enjoy reading. They quickly nail down terminology and master your lessons in literary analysis. For them, critical thinking is fun, and they are eager to try their hand at writing essays.

Predictions for the rest of the class are less certain. Experience tells you that some students will succeed beyond your expectations, while others will slip below them, perhaps by misunderstanding an essay prompt, leaving out a critical element of an argument, or by laboring so carefully and slowly that they leave many multiple-choice questions unanswered. Some are hobbled by a lack of self-confidence. These are the kinds of problems that can be remedied by that most modest of strategies—practice.

It is a proven fact that students perform better on exams when they have practiced the format and have developed confidence in their strategies. As Tim van Gelder explains, "'Practice makes perfect' is a nugget of folk wisdom that has been extensively investigated by science, and it has come out vindicated: You will not get better without practice, and getting really good takes lots of practice. The skills of critical thinking are no exception."[1]

We believe that the AP exam assesses valuable critical thinking and writing skills, and that giving practice exercises tailored specifically to the skills the exam assesses will boost your students' likelihood of success. This book, like the AP exam, draws on imaginative literature dating from the sixteenth century on by a diversity of writers working in a variety of genres. There are five hundred multiple-choice questions based on thirty-eight poetry and prose selections; ten essay questions—four poetry essay questions, four prose essay questions, and two open essay questions—each with two sample responses and comments; and two full-length practice tests. All are printed on easily reproducible masters.

Each of the multiple-choice passages is designed to take about fifteen to twenty minutes for students to complete. In the beginning, speed is not as critical as accuracy; with practice, your students will go faster. You can use passages early in the year to assess students' abilities and to begin to build their familiarity with the kinds of questions that will be on the exam in May. Especially in the beginning, allow students to share their reasoning for their answers and discuss with their classmates how they arrived at them. It is this reasoning capability that is being tested, after all.

For essay prompts, early practice is also critical, even though your students are only starting to master the skills they will need. Here, too, start slowly. In the beginning, you might have students discuss their

---

[1] Tim van Gelder, "Teaching Critical Thinking: Some Lessons from Cognitive Science," College Teaching 53.1 (2005), Questia, 30 Apr. 2008. http://www.questiaschool.com/PM.qst?a=o&d=5008899021.

ideas before (or instead of) writing. They should be able to articulate what the question is asking them to do before they begin to outline their essay, a step crucial to success. Specific prompts can be scheduled to reinforce your lessons and help you assess whether your students are transferring their understanding to other literary works.

There are many other ideas for classroom use. You might split up essay tasks. During one class period, ask students to mark up the prompt and discuss strategies. You could spend another period brainstorming and planning an essay, perfecting an intro, or writing just one body paragraph. Using one of the multiple-choice passages, try asking students to create essay prompts for the selection. This is a valuable exercise because attention to wording leads to astuteness in reading essay prompts. You can also ask students to create multiple-choice questions for the essay passages. Students gain added insight as they consider how to design such questions and as they critique them for usability.

Tim Averill, College Board AP instructor and veteran AP English teacher, suggests that students complete a multiple-choice passage individually; then, in groups, agree on a common answer set by explaining their reasoning and listening to others' analysis. This is the most productive part of the exercise, as students are forced to explain their reasoning and listen to others explain their choices. Finally, the whole class agrees on one answer set, once again refining their critical thinking skills. Makes a great sub plan!

Perrine's Literature: Structure, Sound, and Sense by Thomas R. Arp and Greg Johnson brings together an enormous collection of fiction, poetry, and drama and presents the elements of literature. Concentrating on close reading and literary analysis, it is an excellent anthology for an AP English literature course. *Classroom Practice Exercises* is a comprehensive, focused AP preparation book. A compendium of practice materials, it will pique students' curiosity while challenging them appropriately. The passages are fresh and entertaining, having been selected for their complexity and stylishness, not their free copyright status. Our hope is that *Classroom Practice Exercises* will supply teachers with rich and appealing materials to help their students develop the critical thinking and writing skills needed for success on the AP exam.

The companion volume, *Fast Track to a 5,* is designed for students to use on their own. It explains how the test is set up and scored and contains a thorough review of tone, annotation, and terminology. It offers students strategies for test taking, including how to tackle both the multiple-choice section and the essays. There are sample essays with scoring guidelines and comments. A diagnostic test and two practice tests, are accompanied by detailed explanations for the multiple-choice questions, scoring guidelines for the essay questions, and a worksheet for calculating AP scores and grades. The goal is to help students make the best use of their time as they prepare for the exam.

Part I

Multiple-Choice Questions

Reading 1: Excerpt from "The Lottery" by Shirley Jackson

QUESTIONS 1–14. Carefully read the passage, the end of the short story, before choosing your answers.

Mr. Graves opened the slip of paper and there was a general sigh through the crowd as he held it up and everyone could see that it was blank. Nancy and Bill, Jr., opened theirs at the same time, and both beamed and laughed, turning around to the crowd and holding their slips of paper above their heads. 5

"Tessie," Mr. Summers said. There was a pause, and then Mr. Summers looked at Bill Hutchinson, and Bill unfolded his paper and showed it. It was blank.

"It's Tessie," Mr. Summers said, and his voice was hushed. "Show us her paper, Bill." 10

Bill Hutchinson went over to his wife and forced the slip of paper out of her hand. It had a black spot on it, the black spot Mr. Summers had made the night before with the heavy pencil in the coal-company office. Bill Hutchinson held it up, and there was a stir in the crowd. 15

"All right, folks," Mr. Summers said. "Let's finish quickly."

Although the villagers had forgotten the ritual and lost the original black box, they still remembered to use stones. The pile of stones the boys had made earlier was ready; there were stones on the ground with the blowing scraps of paper that had 20 come out of the box. Mrs. Delacroix selected a stone so large she had to pick it up with both hands and turned to Mrs. Dunbar. "Come on," she said. "Hurry up."

Mrs. Dunbar had small stones in both hands, and she said, gasping for breath, "I can't run at all. You'll have to go ahead 25 and I'll catch up with you."

The children had stones already, and someone gave little Davy Hutchinson a few pebbles.

Tessie Hutchinson was in the center of a cleared space by now, and she held her hands out desperately as the villagers 30 moved in on her. "It isn't fair," she said. A stone hit her on the side of the head.

Old Man Warner was saying, "Come on, come on, everyone." Steve Adams was in front of the crowd of villagers, with Mrs. Graves beside him. 35

"It isn't fair, it isn't right," Mrs. Hutchinson screamed, and then they were upon her.

1. In the passage, ritualistic actions are shown in a manner that could best be described as
   (A) blind
   (B) opportunistic
   (C) clever
   (D) sagacious
   (E) entertaining

2. When little Davy Hutchinson is given a few pebbles, the reader feels
   (A) relieved
   (B) somewhat tricked
   (C) happily noninvolved
   (D) cautiously optimistic
   (E) blatantly misled

3. The fact that Mrs. Dunbar is gasping and out of breath shows
   (A) refusal
   (B) that the aphorism "with age goes wisdom" is often incorrect
   (C) cultural passivity
   (D) certain positive aspects
   (E) disobedience

4. At the end of the passage (line 36), Tessie says, "It isn't fair." This is a prime example of
   (A) understatement
   (B) hyperbole
   (C) kinesthesia
   (D) foreboding
   (E) futility

5. The tone of Jackson's story is best described as
   (A) contemplative
   (B) reflective
   (C) matter-of-fact
   (D) iconoclastic
   (E) facetious

6. An underlying theme of the story is
   (A) stoning is cruel and brutal
   (B) violence takes place anywhere all the people are uneducated
   (C) acts of irrationality can be committed by ordinary people
   (D) clear thinking always trumps mob rule
   (E) good wins over evil

7. The black box is symbolic of
   (A) hope for the future
   (B) happiness that results from change
   (C) the villagers' inability to change
   (D) a happy tradition
   (E) stasis

8. Mrs. Delacroix was friendly to Tessie at the beginning of the story. The fact that she rushes at her with a large stone "she had to pick up with both hands" (lines 21–22) shows
   (A) irony
   (B) resistance
   (C) hope
   (D) flattery
   (E) gluttony

9. Shirley Jackson highlights humankind's capacity to victimize even family and friends to explicate
   (A) the beneficial aspects of humankind
   (B) the value of ancient customs
   (C) the benefit of sacrifice
   (D) a symbol of victimization
   (E) the danger of adherence to norms

10. Because the men pick for their families and the women are treated as subservient, Tessie objects to the method of drawing. This
    (A) stresses the importance of women in society
    (B) reveals the true nature of society
    (C) highlights a negative aspect of patriarchal societies
    (D) shows that Tessie is loved
    (E) shows that Tessie is unloved

11. "The Lottery" is a
    (A) parable
    (B) fabliau
    (C) poem
    (D) tableau
    (E) novella

12. "Although the villagers had forgotten the ritual and lost the original black box, they still remembered to use stones" (lines 17–18) is Jackson's commentary on
    (A) money in society
    (B) the rigors of society
    (C) hope in society
    (D) death in society
    (E) tradition in society

13. "The pile of stones the boys had made earlier was ready" (lines 18–19) shows that the people in Jackson's town want all of the following EXCEPT
    (A) the ritual to persist
    (B) blind adherence to the ritual
    (C) the younger generation to get on board with respect to the town's practices
    (D) the ritual to advance and prevail
    (E) a time when the ritual exists no longer

14. "Bill Hutchinson went over to his wife and forced the slip of paper out of her hand" (lines 11–12) shows
    (A) the unity of Hutchinson's family
    (B) the depth of the Hutchinson family's conviction
    (C) hope for the future
    (D) an utter disregard for human decency
    (E) the senselessness of nonrational adherence to patrimony

See page 130 for the answers to this set of questions.

READING 2: "SAILING TO BYZANTIUM" BY WILLIAM BUTLER YEATS

QUESTIONS 15–29. Carefully read the poem before choosing your answers.

That is no country for old men. The young
In one another's arms, birds in the trees
—Those dying generations—at their song,
The salmon-falls, the mackerel-crowded seas,
Fish, flesh, or fowl, commend all summer long   5
Whatever is begotten, born, and dies.
Caught in that sensual music all neglect
Monuments of unaging intellect.

An aged man is but a paltry thing,
A tattered coat upon a stick, unless   10
Soul clap its hands and sing, and louder sing
For every tatter in its mortal dress,
Nor is there singing school but studying
Monuments of its own magnificence;
And therefore I have sailed the seas and come   15
To the holy city of Byzantium.

O sages standing in God's holy fire
As in the gold mosaic of a wall,
Come from the holy fire, perne in a gyre,
And be the singing-masters of my soul.   20
Consume my heart away; sick with desire
And fastened to a dying animal
It knows not what it is; and gather me
Into the artifice of eternity.

Once out of nature I shall never take   25
My bodily form from any natural thing,
But such a form as Grecian goldsmiths make
Of hammered gold and gold enameling
To keep a drowsy Emperor awake;
Or set upon a golden bough to sing   30
To lords and ladies of Byzantium
Of what is past, or passing, or to come.

15. "That country" (line 1) is
    (A) the past
    (B) the world of poetry and art
    (C) Greece
    (D) the narrator's native land
    (E) the Holy Land

16. The narrator travels to Byzantium to
    (A) seek a sense of permanence and eternity
    (B) visit the "[m]onuments of unaging intellect"
    (C) consult with the sages about art
    (D) visit Greece's goldsmiths
    (E) recover lost vigor and health

17. Of the following, which motif is most significant?
    (A) birds
    (B) the sea
    (C) fire
    (D) song
    (E) art

18. The first stanza includes all of the following EXCEPT
    (A) feminine rhyme
    (B) trochee
    (C) iambic pentameter
    (D) dactyl
    (E) synecdoche

19. The second stanza includes all of the following EXCEPT
    (A) metaphor
    (B) enjambment
    (C) gerund
    (D) double entendre
    (E) loose sentence

20. "Whatever is begotten, born, and dies" (line 6) is a(n)
    (A) noun clause
    (B) adjectival clause
    (C) adverbial clause
    (D) gerund
    (E) participial

21. Who or what is "[c]aught in that sensual music" (line 7)?
    (A) the narrator
    (B) the young (line 1)
    (C) old men (line 1)
    (D) summer (line 5)
    (E) all (line 7)

22. The antecedent of "its" (line 14) is
    (A) coat (line 10)
    (B) stick (line 10)
    (C) soul (line 11)
    (D) mortal dress (line 12)
    (E) singing school (line 13)

23. Who should be "singing-masters" (line 20)?
    (A) sages (line 17)
    (B) God (line 17)
    (C) the narrator
    (D) old men in general
    (E) souls (line 20)

24. All of the following are themes in the poem EXCEPT
    (A) art and artifice
    (B) permanence and decay
    (C) wisdom and intellect
    (D) aging and youth
    (E) love and betrayal

25. Each stanza takes the form of a(n)
    (A) sestina
    (B) octave
    (C) sonnet
    (D) rondeau
    (E) villanelle

26. Overall, the tone of the poem is
    (A) contemplative
    (B) pleading
    (C) pedantic
    (D) despairing
    (E) triumphant

27. The narrator wants to be
    (A) remembered
    (B) eternal
    (C) successful
    (D) erudite
    (E) inspired

28. The antecedent of "It" in line 23 is
    (A) sages (line 17)
    (B) God's holy fire (line 17)
    (C) soul (line 20)
    (D) heart (line 21)
    (E) dying animal (line 22)

29. The phrase "Once out of nature" (line 25) most closely means having
    (A) returned to the city
    (B) become an artist
    (C) departed from life
    (D) studied monuments
    (E) exhausted natural resources

See page 130 for the answers to this set of questions.

READING 3: "THE DEATH OF THE BALL TURRET GUNNER" BY RANDALL JARRELL

QUESTIONS 30–41. To explain the title, Jarrell wrote: "A ball turret was a plexiglass sphere set into the belly of a B-17 or B-24 [bomber during World War II], and inhabited by two .50 caliber machine-guns and one man, a short small man. When this gunner tracked with his machine-guns a fighter [plane] attacking from below, he revolved with the turret; hunched in his little sphere, he looked like the fetus in the womb." Carefully read the poem before choosing your answers.

> From my mother's sleep I fell into the State,
> And I hunched in its belly till my wet fur froze.
> Six miles from earth, loosed from its dream of life,
> I woke to black flak and the nightmare fighters.
> When I died they washed me out of the turret with a hose.   5

30. The theme of Jarrell's poem is
    (A) the institutionalized glory of war
    (B) the moral necessity of war
    (C) that repugnant actions often become inappropriate
    (D) that repugnant actions often become appropriate
    (E) hope for the future

31. "From my mother's sleep I fell into the State" (line 1) is an example of
    (A) paradox
    (B) oxymoron
    (C) parody
    (D) euphemism
    (E) synesthesia

32. In line 1, the words "I fell into the State," coupled with the words "From my mother's sleep," suggest the
    (A) idea that mankind will not sin in war
    (B) brightness of the past
    (C) justification of all war
    (D) idea that mankind knowingly and unknowingly sins in war
    (E) idea that war is not hell

33. Jarrell's capitalization of the word "State" in line 1 suggests
    (A) new orderly government systems
    (B) a new state of mind
    (C) the peaceful state of his mother's womb
    (D) the bureaucratic system present in war
    (E) a government utopia

34. In line 2, "And I hunched in its belly till my wet fur froze," the grammatical antecedent to "its" is
    (A) the mother
    (B) the ball turret
    (C) the gunner
    (D) the state
    (E) the fur

35. The phrase in line 2, "till my wet fur froze," should
    (A) not be taken literally, as the speaker was surely not wearing a warm jacket
    (B) not be taken literally, as it was very warm in the ball turret
    (C) not be taken figuratively, as it produces promising images
    (D) be taken figuratively, as the speaker is taking on the entire world
    (E) be taken figuratively, as the speaker takes on attributes of a small animal

36. "Six miles from earth, loosed from its dream of life" (line 3) shares the speaker's belief that
    (A) life is never meaningless
    (B) hope often springs eternal
    (C) nothing good will ever happen
    (D) the speaker's earthly dreams of a rich full life will be cut off
    (E) the speaker's illusions of a pitiful life will be cut off

37. The term "black flak" (line 4) suggests
    (A) a mimetic for the sounds of war
    (B) sanguinity in the midst of war
    (C) jeopardy in the time of war
    (D) trust for the time of peace
    (E) the ebony color of the airplane

38. Line 4, "I woke to black flak and the nightmare fighters," is unsettling because
    (A) one usually forgets bad dreams
    (B) the normality of the speaker's dream sequence is emphasized
    (C) shattering shells do not wake the speaker
    (D) one usually forgets nightmares
    (E) one usually awakes *from* a bad dream but this speaker awoke *to* a nightmare

39. The entire five lines of the poem regard everything in war as a time indicative of
    I. a fierceness that is miasmatic and finical
    II. something most horrific, where birth becomes death and death is the only reality and release
    III. a life that is merely a dream of earth, while realization is a "nightmare"
    (A) I only
    (B) II only
    (C) I and II only
    (D) III only
    (E) I, II, and III

40. "When I died they washed me out of the turret with a hose" (line 5) shows that the author believes
    (A) the gunner's plight is that he witnesses and acknowledges the reality
    (B) the rest of the world has simply been washed away
    (C) the true survivor's voice has been denied
    (D) the ball turret itself has been shattered and exists no more
    (E) the hose was a lifeline

41. There are by actual count three distinct sentences in this five-line poem, and each centers on one idea. These ideas, enumerated as they appear in sequence, are
    (A) hope, despair, satisfaction
    (B) abortion, anger, dream
    (C) birth, war, death
    (D) faith, hope, charity
    (E) sociology, philosophy, religion

See page 130 for the answers to this set of questions.

READING 4: EXCERPT FROM *TRYING TO FIND CHINATOWN* BY DAVID HENRY HWANG

QUESTIONS 42-54. Carefully read the passage, a monologue by the protagonist near the end of the play, before choosing your answers.

RONNIE: What—you think if I deny the importance of my race, I'm nobody? There're worlds out there, worlds you haven't even begun to understand. Open your eyes. Hear with your ears.

He holds his violin at chest level, does not attempt to play 5
during the following monologue. As he speaks, a montage of
rock and jazz tracks fades in and out over the house speakers,
bringing to life the styles of music he describes.

I concede—it was called a fiddle long ago—but that was
even before the birth of jazz. When the hollering in the 10
fields, the rank injustice of human bondage, the struggle
of God's children against the plagues of the devil's white
man, when all these boiled up into that bittersweet brew,
called by later generations, the blues. That's when
fiddlers like Son Sims held their chin rests at their chests 15
and sawed away like the hillbillies still do today. And with
the coming of ragtime appeared the pioneer Stuff Smith,
who sang as he stroked the catgut, with his raspy Louis
Armstrong voice—gruff and sweet like the timbre of
horsehair riding south below the fingerboard, and who 20
finally sailed for Europe to find ears that would hear.
Europe—where Stephane Grapelli initialed a magical
French violin, to be passed from generation to
generation—first he, to Jean-Luc Ponty, then Ponty to
Didier Lockwood. Listening to Grapelli play "A 25
Nightingale Sang in Berkeley Square" is to understand
not only the song of birds, but also how they learn to fly,
fall in love on the wing, and finally falter one day, to wait
for darkness beneath a London street lamp. And Ponty,
he showed us how the modern violin man can 30
accompany the shadow of his own lead lines, which
cascade, one over another, into some netherworld
beyond the range of human hearing. Joe Venuti, Noel
Pointer, Svend Asmussen. Even the Kronos Quartet with
their arrangement of "Purple Haze." Now, tell me, could 35
any legacy be more rich, more crowded with mythology
and heroes to inspire pride? What can I say if the
banging of a gong or the clinking of a pickax on the
Transcontinental Railroad fails to move me even as much
as one note, played through the violin MIDI controller of 40
Michael Urbaniak?

Ronnie puts his violin to his chin, begins to play a jazz
composition of his own invention.

Does it have to sound like Chinese opera before people
like you decide I know who I am?   45

42. The sentence that begins "When the hollering in the fields" (lines
    10–14) is a
    (A) declarative sentence
    (B) sentence fragment
    (C) periodic sentence
    (D) loose sentence
    (E) complex-compound sentence

43. The phrase "bittersweet brew" (line 13) most closely refers to
    (A) racism
    (B) the American melting pot
    (C) a type of music
    (D) an alcoholic drink
    (E) the anger of the oppressed

44. The passage is primarily a(n)
    (A) concession that the violin was not first used by jazz musicians
    (B) tribute to the violin's versatility and musical significance
    (C) historical report of the violin
    (D) plea for understanding the place of the violin in musical groups
    (E) comparison of types of violin musical styles

45. The violin is compared to all of the following EXCEPT
    (A) the human voice
    (B) the banging of a gong
    (C) the act of learning to fly
    (D) the song of birds
    (E) going to Hell

46. The passage is organized by
    (A) types of violins
    (B) low to high culture
    (C) phases of mastering the violin
    (D) concrete to abstract notions of music
    (E) stages in the evolution of violin music

47. What or who is "gruff and sweet" (line 19)?
    (A) Stuff Smith
    (B) ragtime music
    (C) the fingerboard of a violin
    (D) catgut
    (E) Stuff Smith's voice

48. The phrase "passed from generation to generation" (lines 23–24)
    refers to
    (A) passing musical techniques from a master to an apprentice
        player
    (B) the wisdom that elders pass on to the young
    (C) music that has evolved over time
    (D) handing down a valuable instrument from one musician to
        another
    (E) leaving the next generation the right to experiment with music

49. "Listening to Grapelli" (line 25) is a(n)
    (A) infinitive phrase
    (B) verb plus prepositional phrase
    (C) present participle phrase
    (D) adverb phrase
    (E) gerund phrase

50. The line "not only the song of birds . . ." (line 27) demonstrates
    (A) the depth of meaning violin music holds for Ronnie
    (B) that music transcends speech
    (C) Ronnie's skills as a violinist
    (D) an advanced stage of violin mastery
    (E) the power of love for music

51. The phrase "accompany the shadow of his own lead lines" (line 31) most closely pertains to
    (A) the companionship among violin masters
    (B) the phenomenon of envisioning one's own death
    (C) accepting the superiority of a master violinist
    (D) corresponding notes played simultaneously on the violin
    (E) allowing another violinist to set the playing pace

52. What cascades "into some netherworld" (line 32)?
    (A) the violinist's spirits
    (B) birds
    (C) the audience, as it responds to the violin
    (D) the notes of the violin
    (E) a moral abyss

53. The question "could any legacy be more rich, more crowded with mythology and heroes to inspire pride" (lines 35–37)
    (A) returns to a previous topic in the monologue
    (B) shifts to a new topic
    (C) sums up preceding ideas
    (D) challenges Ronnie's interlocutor to deny his assertions
    (E) synthesizes opposing ideas in the passage

54. The tone of the excerpt is primarily
    (A) hostile
    (B) contemplative
    (C) moody
    (D) nostalgic
    (E) urgent

See page 130 for the answers to this set of questions.

READING 5: "IMAGINE" BY JOHN LENNON

QUESTIONS 55–67. Carefully read the song lyrics before choosing your answers.

```
Imagine there's no heaven
It's easy if you try
No hell below us
Above us only sky
Imagine all the people                    5
Living for today . . .

Imagine there's no countries
It isn't hard to do
Nothing to kill or die for
And no religion too                        10
Imagine all the people
Living life in peace . . .

You may say I'm a dreamer
But I'm not the only one
I hope someday you'll join us              15
And the world will be as one

Imagine no possessions
I wonder if you can
No need for greed or hunger
A brotherhood of man                       20
Imagine all the people
Sharing all the world . . .

You may say I'm a dreamer
But I'm not the only one
I hope someday you'll join us              25
And the world will live as one
```

55. This work uses the poetic stanza called the
    (A) ballad
    (B) quatrain
    (C) heroic couplet
    (D) octave
    (E) terza rima

56. The poem deals with
    (A) the importance of religion giving humans a place in the spiritual universe
    (B) the importance of science denying humans a place in the physical universe
    (C) a humanistic view denying humans a place in the spiritual universe
    (D) an anti-socialist view of humans in the universe
    (E) the joyous redundancy of scientific thought

57. One word that best sums up the poem is
    (A) nihilistic
    (B) socialistic
    (C) religious
    (D) quagmire
    (E) rapine

58. Lennon urges his listeners to create a world that is
    (A) united and fit to live in
    (B) disassociated and not fit to live in
    (C) conceived for decay
    (D) hated and fit for the inevitable
    (E) established for an ethnic realm fit to live in

59. The general tone of the poem emphasizes a
    (A) denial of nescience
    (B) poignant innocence
    (C) petition to establish a monarchy
    (D) disdain for common people
    (E) denial of utopia

60. The words "no heaven"(line 1), "No hell" (line 3), and "Imagine all
    the people / Living for today" (lines 5–6) suggest living life
    (A) not for the moment only
    (B) by procrastinating
    (C) never hedonistically
    (D) without delight
    (E) for the moment only

61. In lines 10–12, "And no religion too / Imagine all the people /
    Living life in peace," the word "too" suggests moving along as
    (A) with countries
    (B) toward religion
    (C) toward science
    (D) with no countries
    (E) with singing

62. The major themes of the poem are
    (A) religion, government, and dreams
    (B) philosophy, science, and culture
    (C) love, hate, and death
    (D) help, money, and love
    (E) truancy, fairness, and laughter

63. The poem is addressed to
    (A) Beatles fans
    (B) all the realists of the world
    (C) all human beings
    (D) the world's scientists
    (E) all the religions of the world

64. In the song, Lennon invites the reader to share his vision of a
    world that
    (A) emphasizes religion
    (B) is not brimming with monetary luxury
    (C) is filled with evil
    (D) is devoid of possessions, countries, and causes
    (E) seeks only possessions

65. The word "imagine" is repeated six times in the poem. Each time it
    is used, it is the initial word in the poetic sentence. This suggests
    that the audience is being
    (A) directly and formally addressed
    (B) admonished
    (C) appeased
    (D) rejected
    (E) warned

66. Lennon uses the word "imagine" in each of the six references as an
    example of
    (A) alliteration
    (B) apostrophe
    (C) anaphora
    (D) repetition ad nauseam
    (E) consonance

67. The poem's overarching theme is that
    (A) the world is headed quickly to perdition
    (B) the world can never change
    (C) the world is predestined for deficiency
    (D) seemingly improbable ideas can succeed against great odds
    (E) seemingly improbable ideas can never succeed

See page 130 for the answers to this set of questions.

READING 6: "CINDERELLA" BY ANNE SEXTON

QUESTIONS 68–79. Carefully read the poem before choosing your answers.

You always read about it:
the plumber with twelve children
who wins the Irish Sweepstakes.
From toilets to riches.
That story.   5

Or the nursemaid,
some luscious sweet from Denmark
who captures the oldest son's heart.
From diapers to Dior.
That story.   10

Or a milkman who serves the wealthy,
eggs, cream, butter, yogurt, milk,
the white truck like an ambulance
who goes into real estate
and makes a pile.   15
From homogenized to martinis at lunch.

Or the charwoman
who is on the bus when it cracks up
and collects enough from the insurance.
From mops to Bonwit Teller.   20
That story.

Once
the wife of a rich man was on her deathbed
and she said to her daughter Cinderella:
Be devout. Be good. Then I will smile   25
down from heaven in the seam of a cloud.
The man took another wife who had
two daughters, pretty enough
but with hearts like blackjacks.
Cinderella was their maid.   30
She slept on the sooty hearth each night
and walked around looking like Al Jolson.
Her father brought presents home from town,
jewels and gowns for the other women
but the twig of a tree for Cinderella.   35
She planted that twig on her mother's grave
and it grew to a tree where a white dove sat.
Whenever she wished for anything the dove
would drop it like an egg upon the ground.
The bird is important, my dears, so heed him.   40

Next came the ball, as you all know.
It was a marriage market.
The prince was looking for a wife.

All but Cinderella were preparing
and gussying up for the big event.   45
Cinderella begged to go too.
Her stepmother threw a dish of lentils
into the cinders and said: Pick them
up in an hour and you shall go.
The white dove brought all his friends;   50
all the warm wings of the fatherland came,
and picked up the lentils in a jiffy.
No, Cinderella, said the stepmother,
you have no clothes and cannot dance.
That's the way with stepmothers.   55

Cinderella went to the tree at the grave
and cried forth like a gospel singer:
Mama! Mama! My turtledove,
send me to the prince's ball!
The bird dropped down a golden dress   60
and delicate little gold slippers.
Rather a large package for a simple bird.
So she went. Which is no surprise.
Her stepmother and sisters didn't
recognize her without her cinder face   65
and the prince took her hand on the spot
and danced with no other the whole day.

As nightfall came she thought she'd better
get home. The prince walked her home
and she disappeared into the pigeon house   70
and although the prince took an axe and broke
it open she was gone. Back to her cinders.
These events repeated themselves for three days.
However on the third day the prince
covered the palace steps with cobbler's wax   75
and Cinderella's gold shoe stuck upon it.
Now he would find whom the shoe fit
and find his strange dancing girl for keeps.
He went to their house and the two sisters
were delighted because they had lovely feet.   80
The eldest went into a room to try the slipper on
but her big toe got in the way so she simply
sliced it off and put on the slipper.
The prince rode away with her until the white dove
told him to look at the blood pouring forth.   85
That is the way with amputations.
They just don't heal up like a wish.
The other sister cut off her heel
but the blood told as blood will.
The prince was getting tired.   90
He began to feel like a shoe salesman.
But he gave it one last try.
This time Cinderella fit into the shoe
like a love letter into its envelope.

> At the wedding ceremony   95
> the two sisters came to curry favor
> and the white dove pecked their eyes out.
> Two hollow spots were left
> like soup spoons.
>
> Cinderella and the prince   100
> lived, they say, happily ever after,
> like two dolls in a museum case
> never bothered by diapers or dust,
> never arguing over the timing of an egg,
> never telling the same story twice,   105
> never getting a middle-aged spread,
> their darling smiles pasted on for eternity.
> Regular Bobbsey Twins.
> That story.

68. The last line of the first stanza (line 5)
    (A) establishes the narrator's ethos of authority
    (B) raises doubts that Cinderella will get the prince
    (C) undercuts the seriousness of the previous lines
    (D) establishes pathos for the poor plumber
    (E) interrupts the narrative flow

69. The phrase "luscious sweet" (line 7) is an example of a(n)
    (A) double entendre
    (B) personification
    (C) oxymoron
    (D) metonymy
    (E) allusion

70. The poem is an example of a(n)
    (A) mock epic
    (B) epistolary ballad
    (C) feminist elegy
    (D) satiric parable
    (E) ironic retelling

71. The line "From mops to Bonwit Teller" (line 20) is an example of a(n)
    (A) mixed metaphor
    (B) set of antonyms
    (C) oxymoron
    (D) political allusion
    (E) paired analogy

72. The phrase "gussying up" (line 45) is an example of
    (A) a colloquialism
    (B) a recurring motif
    (C) a cacophony
    (D) a pastoral reference
    (E) irony

73. The humor of the phrase "cried forth like a gospel singer" (line 57)
    comes from
    (A) playful understatement
    (B) a sarcastic truism
    (C) satirical allusions
    (D) incongruous diction
    (E) droll understatement

74. "Mama! Mama!" (line 58) is an example of a(n)
    (A) appositive
    (B) apostrophe
    (C) aphorism
    (D) dramatic aside
    (E) denouement

75. In their last lines, many of the stanzas contain a(n)
    (A) personification
    (B) biased statement
    (C) didacticism
    (D) authorial aside
    (E) exhortation

76. At the end of the eighth stanza, the line "like a love letter into its
    envelope" is a(n)
    (A) zeugma
    (B) antithesis
    (C) antonym
    (D) antecedent
    (E) simile

77. The final stanza includes an example of a(n)
    (A) oxymoron
    (B) antistrophe
    (C) anaphora
    (D) synecdoche
    (E) chiasmus

78. The tone of the poem is one of
    (A) haughty derision
    (B) playful irony
    (C) satiric mockery
    (D) outright condemnation
    (E) pedantic authority

79. Based on the subtext of this poem, the author seems to have
    sympathy for
    (A) feminist ideology
    (B) Marxist ideology
    (C) human rights
    (D) the underdog
    (E) nonconformists

See page 130 for the answers to this set of questions.

READING 7: "A VALEDICTION: FORBIDDING MOURNING" BY JOHN DONNE

QUESTIONS 80–94. Carefully read the poem before choosing your answers.

As virtuous men pass mildly away,
    And whisper to their souls to go,
Whilst some of their sad friends do say,
    The breath goes now, and some say no:

So let us melt, and make no noise,   5
    No tear-floods, nor sigh-tempests move;
'Twere profanation of our joys
    To tell the laity our love.

Moving of th' earth brings harms and fears;
    Men reckon what it did and meant;   10
But trepidation of the spheres,
    Though greater far, is innocent.

Dull sublunary lovers' love
    (Whose soul is sense) cannot admit
Absence, because it doth remove   15
    Those things which elemented it.

But we, by a love so much refined
    That ourselves know not what it is,
Inter-assurèd of the mind,
    Care less, eyes, lips, and hands to miss.   20

Our two souls, therefore, which are one,
    Though I must go, endure not yet
A breach, but an expansion,
    Like gold to airy thinness beat.

If they be two, they are two so   25
    As stiff twin compasses are two;
Thy soul, the fixed foot, makes no show
    To move, but doth, if th' other do.

And though it in the center sit,
    Yet when the other far doth roam,   30
It leans and harkens after it,
    And grows erect as that comes home.

Such wilt thou be to me, who must,
    Like th' other foot, obliquely run;
Thy firmness makes my circle just,   35
    And makes me end where I begun.

80. The poem shows the precise rhyme scheme knows as
    (A) blank verse
    (B) ballad
    (C) terza rima
    (D) rhyme royal
    (E) ode

81. The poem suggests that Donne's love for his wife and hers for him is
    (A) purely sensual and sexual
    (B) physical, not spiritual
    (C) a love of the mind as well as the body
    (D) about to end
    (E) fated to end

82. The entire poem exemplifies
    (A) the Petrarchan sonnet
    (B) the poetic parable
    (C) the Elizabethan pastoral
    (D) the metaphysical conceit
    (E) stream of consciousness

83. The lovers are likened to moving planetary bodies that are
    (A) chaotic
    (B) natural disasters
    (C) peaceful and calm
    (D) out of order
    (E) irrelevant

84. The poem suggests that the two lovers are their own self-sustaining universe because
    (A) they have no need of anyone else
    (B) they are made imperfect by their love
    (C) they know how to use a compass
    (D) they look at the moon together
    (E) they will soon divorce

85. In lines 22–23, "endure not yet / A breach," the word "yet" hints that
    (A) there will never be a breach, not even with death
    (B) with death eventually there will be a breach
    (C) love will find a way
    (D) hope springs eternal
    (E) love will never rupture

86. The theme of this poem is best expressed as a separation that
    (A) must cause grief
    (B) does not need consolation or fortitude
    (C) is part of the nature and completeness of the lovers' world
    (D) is not sacred
    (E) is not a mystical force

87. Line 24, "Like gold to airy thinness beat," is an example of
    (A) metaphor
    (B) simile
    (C) oxymoron
    (D) alliteration
    (E) paradox

88. In the opening, "As virtuous men pass mildly away, / And whisper to their souls to go" (lines 1–2), Donne is describing
    (A) a love that eventually ends
    (B) a hope that eventually stops
    (C) a journey that eventually ends
    (D) a death that happens peacefully
    (E) a rage against death

89. In line 16, "Those things which elemented it," Donne uses the verb "elemented" to mean
    (A) separated
    (B) removed
    (C) composed
    (D) expunged
    (E) eliminated

90. In using the "twin compasses" (line 26), Donne does not compare the perfection of his love to a traditional object, but to two things so different that we feel an anomaly. This image is an example of
    (A) screed
    (B) malediction
    (C) arrogance
    (D) conceit
    (E) voracity

91. The use of the pronoun "it" in the eighth stanza, in lines 29 and 31, refers metaphorically to
    (A) the poet
    (B) the poet's wife
    (C) the compass that always points north
    (D) the dead preacher
    (E) the part of the compass that moves

92. Lines 33–34, "Such wilt thou be to me, who must, / Like th' other foot, obliquely run," suggest that Donne is asking his wife
    (A) to remain at the center
    (B) to go with him
    (C) for a divorce
    (D) to learn how to use a compass
    (E) to realize that separation ends things

93. The poem's ending, "Thy firmness makes my circle just, / And makes me end where I begun" (lines 35–36), means that a compass
    (A) must always point north
    (B) works only if one foot remains centered firmly
    (C) is not a good item to compare to love
    (D) helps in understanding divorce
    (E) symbolizes hatred

94. In lines 7–8, "'Twere profanation of our joys / To tell the laity our love," Donne says that the love he and his wife have
    (A) can never really be understood by others
    (B) can never be understood because it is only spiritual
    (C) can never be understood because it is purely physical
    (D) cannot exist
    (E) can exist because it is only platonic

See page 131 for the answers to this set of questions.

READING 8: "LOST SISTER" BY CATHY SONG

QUESTIONS 95–106. Carefully read the poem before choosing your answers.

1
In China,
even the peasants
named their first daughters
Jade–
the stone that in the far fields   5
could moisten the dry season,
could make men move mountains
for the healing green of the inner hills
glistening like slices of winter melon.

And the daughters were grateful: 10
they never left home.
To move freely was a luxury
stolen from them at birth.
Instead, they gathered patience,
learning to walk in shoes   15
the size of teacups,
without breaking–
the arc of their movements
as dormant as the rooted willow,
as redundant as the farmyard hens.   20
But they traveled far
in surviving,
learning to stretch the family rice,
to quiet the demons,
the noisy stomachs.   25

2
There is a sister
across the ocean,
who relinquished her name,
diluting jade green
with the blue of the Pacific.   30
Rising with a tide of locusts,
she swarmed with others
to inundate another shore.
In America,
there are many roads   35
and women can stride along with men.

But in another wilderness,
the possibilities,
the loneliness,
can strangulate like jungle vines.   40
The meager provisions and sentiments
of once belonging–
fermented roots, Mah-Jongg tiles and firecrackers–

set but a flimsy household
in a forest of nightless cities.   45
A giant snake rattles above,
spewing black clouds into your kitchen.
Dough-faced landlords
slip in and out of your keyholes,
making claims you don't understand,   50
tapping into your communication systems
of laundry lines and restaurant chains.

You find you need China:
your one fragile identification,
a jade link   55
handcuffed to your wrist.
You remember your mother
who walked for centuries,
footless—
and like her,   60
you have left no footprints,
but only because
there is an ocean in between,
the unremitting space of your rebellion.

95. The first section (lines 1–25) includes all of the following EXCEPT
     (A) onomatopoeia
     (B) enjambment
     (C) hyperbole
     (D) appositive
     (E) simile

96. The tone of the poem can best be described as
     (A) tentative
     (B) nostalgic
     (C) nonchalant
     (D) charitable
     (E) refined

97. The word "sister" in line 26 refers to
     (A) the narrator's sister in China
     (B) immigrant women from China
     (C) peasant daughters
     (D) women with traditional names
     (E) Chinese women who bound their feet

98. The phrase "diluting jade green" (line 29) could connote all of the
     following EXCEPT
     (A) losing one's identity
     (B) diluting racial purity
     (C) rejecting China's influence
     (D) forgetting Chinese culture
     (E) following Chinese tradition

99. Which of the following pairs has phrases that do NOT relate to each other?
    (A) "make men move mountains" (line 7); "women can stride along with men" (line 36)
    (B) "patience" (line 14); "rebellion" (line 64)
    (C) "teacups" (line 16); "locusts" (line 31)
    (D) "dormant as the rooted willow" (line 19); "strangulate like jungle roots" (line 40)
    (E) "stretch the family rice" (line 23); "laundry lines and restaurant chains" (line 52)

100. The poem moves from
    (A) past, to present, to future
    (B) China, to America, to China
    (C) loss, to hope, to disillusionment
    (D) flight, to arrival, to return
    (E) heritage, to legacy, to heirloom

101. Which of the following lines best expresses the theme of the poem?
    (A) "And the daughters were grateful" (line 10)
    (B) "In America, / there are many roads" (lines 34–35)
    (C) "the loneliness, / can strangulate like jungle vines" (lines 39–40)
    (D) "You find you need China" (line 53)
    (E) "you have left no footprints," (line 61)

102. For the narrator, the details of "fermented roots, Mah-Jongg tiles and firecrackers" (line 43) serve as
    (A) superficial markers of ethnic culture
    (B) forms of entertainment from China
    (C) strong links to ancient China
    (D) effective bulwarks against forgetting China
    (E) examples of painful memories of China

103. The organization of the poem into sections marked "1" and "2" most importantly serves to
    (A) separate past from present
    (B) announce a shift in mood
    (C) create the sense of two different poems
    (D) heighten contrasts between Chinese sisters
    (E) reinforce the theme of separation

104. The poem portrays the immigrant's conflict over the pull of
    (A) dignity versus humiliation
    (B) honor versus betrayal
    (C) freedom versus heritage
    (D) tradition versus modernity
    (E) art versus life

105. The phrase "arc of their movements" (line 18) connotes all of the following EXCEPT the
    (A) need to control one's emotions
    (B) limitations on women's freedom
    (C) Chinese marriage ceremony
    (D) formalized nature of Chinese social rituals
    (E) ritualized movement in traditional Chinese dance

106. As evidenced by this poem, the poet's attitude toward China is
     ultimately
     (A) wistful
     (B) grief-stricken
     (C) worshipful
     (D) derogatory
     (E) laudatory

See page 131 for the answers to this set of questions.

READING 9: "CHRIST CLIMBED DOWN" BY LAWRENCE FERLINGHETTI

QUESTIONS 107–121. Carefully read the poem before choosing your answers.

Christ climbed down
from His bare Tree
this year
and ran away to where
there were no rootless Christmas trees   5
hung with candycanes and breakable stars

Christ climbed down
from His bare Tree
this year
and ran away to where   10
there were no gilded Christmas trees
and no tinsel Christmas trees
and no tinfoil Christmas trees
and no pink plastic Christmas trees
and no gold Christmas trees   15
and no black Christmas trees
and no powderblue Christmas trees
hung with electric candles
and encircled by tin electric trains
and clever cornball relatives   20

Christ climbed down
from His bare Tree
this year
and ran away to where
no intrepid Bible salesman   25
covered the territory
in two-tone cadillacs
and where no Sears Roebuck creches
complete with plastic babe in manger
arrived by parcel post   30
the babe by special delivery
and where no televised Wise Men
praised the Lord Calvert Whiskey

Christ climbed down   35
from His bare Tree
this year
and ran away to where
no fat handshaking stranger
in a red flannel suit
and a fake beard   40
went around passing himself off
as some sort of North Pole saint
crossing the desert to Bethlehem

Pennsylvania

in a Volkswagon sled   45

drawn by rollicking Adirondack reindeer

with German names

and bearing sacks of Humble Gifts

from Saks Fifth Avenue

for everybody's imagined Christ child   50

Christ climbed down

from His bare Tree

this year

and ran away to where

no Bing Crosby carollers   55

groaned of a tight Christmas

and where no Radio City angels

iceskated wingless

thru a winter wonderland

into a jinglebell heaven   60

daily at 8:30

with Midnight Mass matinees

Christ climbed down

from His bare Tree

this year   65

and softly stole away into

some anonymous Mary's womb again

where in the darkest night

of everybody's anonymous soul

He awaits again   70

an unimaginable

and impossibly

Immaculate Reconception

the very craziest

of Second Comings   75

107. The entire poem is
    (A) in favor of blasphemy
    (B) against crass commercialism
    (C) filled with victorious remembrances
    (D) notable for its absence of religious fervor
    (E) notably vacuous

108. In the first six lines of the poem, Ferlinghetti
    (A) denigrates the banal secular trappings that often surround
        religion
    (B) derides all religious ceremonies
    (C) ridicules the true and devoted followers of organized religion
    (D) ridicules Christmas once and for all
    (E) ridicules religion once and for all

109. The phrase "from His bare Tree" (lines 2, 8, 22 , 35, 52, and 64),
     coupled with "rootless Christmas trees / hung with candycanes
     and breakable stars" (lines 5–6) conjures images
     (A) of optimism in a heretical world
     (B) that reduce complicated doctrine to a naïve basis
     (C) that are doctrinaire yet clearly muted
     (D) of the mundane thrust into conflict with the sacred
     (E) that are rather positive and obvious

110. The recurring lines "Christ climbed down / from His bare Tree /
     this year" (for example, lines 1–3) are an example of
     (A) anaphora
     (B) repetition ad nauseam
     (C) epic simile
     (D) epistolary poetry
     (D) ballade

111. The strength of the poem comes from the use in lines 11–17 of
     adjectives that describe different styles of trees. This particular
     use of adjectives reinvigorates
     (A) the true essence of the season
     (B) the author's preference for the secular
     (C) the true religious tranquillity of the season
     (D) the main didactic nature of the argument of the poem
     (E) the secular improvements of the season

112. In the course of his poem, Ferlinghetti moves from using "Tree"
     to using "tree." This shows
     (A) a metaphoric drift from confidence to pessimism
     (B) a symbolic and abject decline from the Cross to the
         Christmas tree
     (C) a physical change from fake to real
     (D) no real change in shift
     (E) a fortunate, significant shift

113. Lines 21–33 are replete with
     (A) positive images of deceit and corruption
     (B) negative images from the sordid world of commerce
     (C) nasty images from the world of childhood
     (D) lovely images of sustaining religious fervor
     (E) loyalty to all religions

114. For the most part, the poet laments
      I. the folk customs surrounding Christmas
     II. the hustle of preparations for the way Christmas should be
     III. the hijacking of Christmas
     (A) I and II only
     (B) I only
     (C) II and III only
     (D) II only
     (E) I, II, and III

115. In line 56, the word "tight" is
 (A) a misprint for the word "night"
 (B) a sarcastic and droll substitute for the word "white"
 (C) an example of hyperbole and a substitute for the word "sight"
 (D) a morose alternative to the word "fight"
 (E) a play on the word "flight"

116. The poet uses "Bible salesman" (line 25), "Sears Roebuck creches" (line 28), "plastic babe in manger" (line 29), and "praised the Lord Calvert Whiskey" (line 33) to magnify the depictions of
 (A) the relics of America in the 1950s
 (B) an advantageous forfeiture of the solemn and the sacred
 (C) the true spirit of Christmas
 (D) the ugly commercialism of Christmas
 (E) the overly introspective nature of the season

117. In " Christmas trees / . . . encircled by tin electric trains / and clever cornball relatives" (lines 17–20), Ferlinghetti
 (A) bashes an absence of familial affability
 (B) builds on participating in Christian fellowship
 (C) eradicates seasonal illness and depression
 (D) makes a purely political statement
 (E) praises family relationships

118. The ideas and images in the fourth stanza, lines 35–50, are meant to
 (A) mix suitably the secular and the sacred
 (B) display the true meaning of the season
 (C) ridicule the stupidity of the amalgamation of disparate myths
 (D) delight in purely religious ambiguity
 (E) show the pleasure of multiculturalism

119. The theme, figurative language, and images in lines 51–62 seem to demonstrate a
 (A) reliance on the wholly religious symbolism of 1950s America
 (B) reliance on the sights and sounds of New York City in the 1950s
 (C) new faith for the future of America after the 1950s
 (D) hope for humans
 (E) destruction of commerce

120. In "and where no Sears Roebuck creches / complete with plastic babe in manger / arrived by parcel post / the babe by special delivery" (lines 28–31), Ferlinghetti contrasts
 (A) modern fake manger scenes and classical creches
 (B) Christ's birth and a postal shipment
 (C) serene happiness and secular sadness
 (D) parcel post and regular mail
 (E) love and money

121. The words "and softly stole away into / some anonymous Mary's womb again" (lines 66–67) show that Ferlinghetti's personal views on the Second Coming are that
    (A) when it happens, we shouldn't look because it will probably not occur ever again
    (B) we should realize it's not possible due to commercialism
    (C) we should look for Christ incognito in everyone we meet
    (D) we should look for a splashy entrance by Christ
    (E) we will never be happy again

See page 131 for the answers to this set of questions.

READING 10: EXCERPT FROM *A MIDSUMMER NIGHT'S DREAM* BY WILLIAM SHAKESPEARE

QUESTIONS 122–136. Carefully read the passage, from Act 2, Scene 1, in which Titania, a fairy queen, confronts Oberon, her lover, before choosing your answers.

TITANIA: These are the forgeries of jealousy;
And never, since the middle summer's spring,
Met we on hill, in dale, forest, or mead,
By paved fountain or by rushy brook,
Or in the beached margent of the sea,   5
To dance our ringlets to the whistling wind,
But with thy brawls thou hast disturb'd our sport.
Therefore the winds, piping to us in vain,
As in revenge, have suck'd up from the sea
Contagious fogs; which, falling in the land,   10
Hath every pelting river made so proud
That they have overborne their continents.
The ox hath therefore stretch'd his yoke in vain,
The ploughman lost his sweat, and the green corn
Hath rotted ere his youth attain'd a beard.   15
The fold stands empty in the drowned field,
And crows are fatted with the murrion flock;
The nine men's morris is fill'd up with mud;
And the quaint mazes in the wanton green,
For lack of tread, are undistinguishable.   20
The human mortals want their winter here;
No night is now with hymn or carol blest.
Therefore the moon (the governess of floods),
Pale in her anger, washes all the air,
That rheumatic diseases do abound.   25
And thorough this distemperature, we see
The seasons alter: hoary-headed frosts
Fall in the fresh lap of the crimson rose,
And on old Hiems' [thin] and icy crown
An odorous chaplet of sweet summer buds   30
Is, as in mockery, set, the spring, the summer,
The childing autumn, angry winter, change
Their wonted liveries, and the mazed world,
By their increase, now knows not which is which.
And this same progeny of evils comes   35
From our debate, from our dissension;
We are their parents and original.

122. The passage demonstrates that Titania is
 (A) euphoric
 (B) wrathful
 (C) mocking
 (D) degrading
 (E) arrogant

123. The rhetorical structure of this speech consists of
     (A) deductive reasoning
     (B) causes and effects
     (C) synthesis
     (D) comparison and contrast
     (E) a litany of stipulations

124. "These are the forgeries . . . disturb'd our sport" (lines 1–7) is
     what type of sentence?
     (A) run-on
     (B) interrogative
     (C) declarative
     (D) periodic
     (E) loose

125. "These are the forgeries of jealousy" (line 1) most closely means
     (A) you have made me jealous
     (B) you are too jealous
     (C) jealousy caused this
     (D) these are examples of jealousy
     (E) these are acceptable reasons to be jealous

126. The phrase "But with" (line 7) means
     (A) without
     (B) yet
     (C) always with
     (D) in addition
     (E) including

127. The phrase "piping to us in vain" (line 8) is a(n)
     (A) gerund phrase
     (B) squinting modifier
     (C) infinitive phrase
     (D) participial phrase
     (E) appositive

128. The word "want" in line 21 means
     (A) find
     (B) desire
     (C) lack
     (D) claim
     (E) lose

129. Lines 23–25 contain a(n)
     (A) compound verb
     (B) appositive
     (C) participial phrase
     (D) adjective clause
     (E) noun clause

130. The details in lines 26–31 indicate that
     (A) Titania has triumphed
     (B) nature approves of its god, Oberon
     (C) the old have become infirm
     (D) the seasons are mixed up
     (E) Titania has deferred to Oberon

131. "[C]hange / Their wonted liveries" (lines 32–33) means
    (A) replace their servants
    (B) change their minds
    (C) demand more respect
    (D) advertise for help
    (E) change their raiment

132. The word "progeny" (line 35) means
    (A) children
    (B) prediction
    (C) creators
    (D) advocates
    (E) predators

133. The meter of this passage is primarily
    (A) iambic pentameter
    (B) trochaic
    (C) sprung
    (D) free verse
    (E) tetrameter

134. The antecedent of "their" in line 34 is
    (A) "rheumatic diseases" (line 25)
    (B) "distemperature" (line 26)
    (C) "The seasons" (line 27)
    (D) "sweet summer buds" (line 30)
    (E) "the mazed world" (line 33)

135. Titania's diction can be described as
    (A) erudite
    (B) majestic
    (C) inscrutable
    (D) quotidian
    (E) esoteric

136. Titania's speech refers to all of the following EXCEPT
    (A) the weather
    (B) the seasons
    (C) farming
    (D) religion
    (E) magic

See page 131 for the answers to this set of questions.

READING 11: EXCERPT FROM "THE CASK OF AMONTILLADO" BY EDGAR ALLAN POE

QUESTIONS 137–151. Carefully read the passage, the end of the story, before choosing your answers.

"I forget your arms."

"A huge human foot d'or, in a field azure; the foot crushes a serpent rampant whose fangs are imbedded in the heel."

"And the motto?"   5

"Nemo me impune lacessit."[1]

"Good!" he said.

The wine sparkled in his eyes and the bells jingled. My own fancy grew warm with the Médoc. We had passed through long walls of piled   10
skeletons, with casks and puncheons intermingling, into the inmost recesses of the catacombs. I paused again, and this time I made bold to seize Fortunato by an arm above the elbow.

"The nitre!" I said; "see, it increases. It hangs   15
like moss upon the vaults. We are below the river's bed. The drops of moisture trickle among the bones. Come, we will go back ere it is too late. Your cough—"

"It is nothing," he said; "let us go on. But first,   20
another draught of the Médoc."

I broke and reached him a flagon of De Grâve. He emptied it at a breath. His eyes flashed with a fierce light. He laughed and threw the bottle upwards with a gesticulation I did not understand.   25

I looked at him in surprise. He repeated the movement—a grotesque one.

"You do not comprehend?" he said.

"Not I," I replied.

"Then you are not of the brotherhood."   30

"How?"

"You are not of the masons."

"Yes, yes," I said; "yes, yes."

"You? Impossible! A mason?"

"A mason," I replied.   35

"A sign," he said, "a sign."

"It is this," I answered, producing from beneath the folds of my *roquelaire* a trowel.

"You jest," he exclaimed, recoiling a few paces. "But let us proceed to the Amontillado."   40

---

[1] No one can provoke me and get away with it.

"Be it so," I said, replacing the tool beneath the cloak and again offering him my arm. He leaned upon it heavily. We continued our route in search of the Amontillado. We passed through a range of low arches, descended, passed on, and descending again, arrived at a deep crypt, in which the foulness of the air caused our flambeaux rather to glow than flame.   45

. . .

"For the love of God, Montresor!"
"Yes," I said, "for the love of God!"   50
But to these words I hearkened in vain for a reply. I grew impatient. I called aloud—
"Fortunato!"
No answer. I called again—
"Fortunato!"   55
No answer still. I thrust a torch through the remaining aperture and let it fall within. There came forth in return only a jingling of the bells. My heart grew sick; it was the dampness of the catacombs that made it so. I hastened to make an end of my   60
labour. I forced the last stone into its position; I plastered it up. Against the new masonry I re-erected the old rampart of bones. For the half of a century no mortal has disturbed them. *In pace requiescat!*[2]   65

137. The word "arms" in line 1 refers to
   (A) Fortunato's upper appendages
   (B) Montresor's upper appendages
   (C) the heraldry of Fortunato
   (D) the heraldry of Montresor
   (E) the base of the wooden cask of wine

138. "Come, we will go back ere it is too late. Your cough—" (lines 18–19) and "It is nothing . . . let us go on" (line 20) stress
   (A) the dampness of the subterranean passage
   (B) a foreshadowing of the denouement
   (C) the portent of the heraldry
   (D) the value of wine
   (E) the worth of monuments

139. Montresor shows that he is an unreliable storyteller because
   (A) he appears to be intoxicated by the Amontillado
   (B) he pretends to be ostentatious and well-to-do
   (C) he does not make known everything about the past
   (D) he is somewhat unable and very unwilling to think clearly
   (E) he is an expert on wine

---

[2] May he rest in peace!

140. Montresor's actions throughout this excerpt allow the reader to conclude that he is
    (A) malicious and maladjusted
    (B) sagacious and fair-minded
    (C) a much better person than Fortunato
    (D) unruffled and open-hearted
    (E) agreeable and benevolent

141. The dialogue in lines 34–37 shows Poe's ability to
    (A) picture the known situation
    (B) emphasize the unexplored
    (C) emphasize the unknown irony
    (D) appreciate and treasure good wine
    (E) understand and value heraldry

142. The picture painted by the words "the foot crushes a serpent rampant whose fangs are imbedded in the heel" (lines 2–4) shows
    (A) the ingenuous retaliatory nature of the story
    (B) the essence of love and admiration
    (C) the optimism for the future with new horizons
    (D) the money spent on wine
    (E) the tempting nature of the cave

143. "We had passed through long walls of piled skeletons, with casks and puncheons intermingling, into the inmost recesses of the catacombs" (lines10–12), combined with "'The nitre!' I said; 'see, it increases. It hangs like moss upon the vaults. We are below the river's bed. The drops of moisture trickle among the bones'" (lines 15–17), adds to the power of the story by
    (A) making no reference to dying
    (B) making implicit allusions to wine
    (C) giving hope to the captive
    (D) making reference to the stench of decay
    (E) showing an absence of revenge

144. In this context, *roquelaire* (line 38) is best understood to mean
    (A) a cloak that reaches to the knees
    (B) a jester's cap that has bells on it
    (C) a holsterlike contraption that hangs from a belt
    (D) a space in the boot or foot covering for storing concealed weapons
    (E) a bottle of expensive wine

145. The word "aperture" (line 57) means
    (A) an adjustable opening in an optical instrument
    (B) a flammable substance similar to a wick
    (C) an opening, such as a hole, gap, or slit
    (D) an enclosure over a shrine
    (E) the stopper in a bottle of wine

146. In line 63, "rampart" refers to
    (A) not being fortified against assault
    (B) an absence of any defence from assault
    (C) something that does not secure safely
    (D) the weak link in the armor
    (E) any defense or bulwark

147. "My heart grew sick; it was the dampness of the catacombs that made it so" (lines 58–60) shows
    I. the narrator's lack of conscience and utter contempt for his victim
    II. the narrator's disgust at himself for his own actions
    III. the depth of the revulsion the perpetrator feels
    (A) I only
    (B) I and II only
    (C) II and III only
    (D) III only
    (E) II only

148. The main characters in this story are named
    (A) Médoc and Amontillado
    (B) DeGrâve and Médoc
    (C) Nemo and Amontillado
    (D) Fortunato and Médoc
    (E) Montresor and Fortunato

149. As the story reaches its climax, "He repeated the movement—a grotesque one" (lines 26–27) and "You do not comprehend?" (line 28) prove
    (A) to be a prophesy
    (B) only slightly ironic
    (C) a lack of fatalism
    (D) inevitable
    (E) to not be a fallacy

150. The mood of the excerpt could be described as
    (A) genteel
    (B) somnambulistic
    (C) whimsical
    (D) fickle
    (E) macabre

151. The entire excerpt details
    (A) the world of wine
    (B) the study of caves
    (C) a keen interest in the hideous and ghastly
    (D) the science of heraldry
    (E) the profession of masonry

See page 131 for the answers to this set of questions.

Reading 12: "Daddy" by Sylvia Plath

Questions 152–163. Carefully read the poem before choosing your answers.

You do not do, you do not do
Any more, black shoe
In which I have lived like a foot
For thirty years, poor and white,
Barely daring to breathe or Achoo.   5

Daddy, I have had to kill you.
You died before I had time—
Marble-heavy, a bag full of God,
Ghastly statue with one grey toe
Big as a Frisco seal   10

And a head in the freakish Atlantic
Where it pours bean green over blue
In the waters off beautiful Nauset.
I used to pray to recover you.
Ach, du.   15

In the German tongue, in the Polish town
Scraped flat by the roller
Of wars, wars, wars.
But the name of the town is common.
My Polack friend   20

Says there are a dozen or two.
So I never could tell where you
Put your foot, your root,
I never could talk to you.
The tongue stuck in my jaw.   25

It stuck in a barb wire snare.
Ich, ich, ich, ich,
I could hardly speak.
I thought every German was you.
And the language obscene   30

An engine, an engine
Chuffing me off like a Jew.
A Jew to Dachau, Auschwitz, Belsen.
I began to talk like a Jew.
I think I may well be a Jew.   35

The snows of the Tyrol, the clear beer of Vienna
Are not very pure or true.
With my gypsy ancestress and my weird luck
And my Taroc pack and my Taroc pack
I may be a bit of a Jew.   40

I have always been scared of *you*,
With your Luftwaffe, your gobbledygoo.
And your neat mustache
And your Aryan eye, bright blue.
Panzer-man, panzer-man, O You—   45

Not God but a swastika
So black no sky could squeak through.
Every woman adores a Fascist,
The boot in the face, the brute
Brute heart of a brute like you.   50

You stand at the blackboard, daddy,
In the picture I have of you,
A cleft in your chin instead of your foot
But no less a devil for that, no not
Any less the black man who   55

Bit my pretty red heart in two.
I was ten when they buried you.
At twenty I tried to die
And get back, back, back to you.
I thought even the bones would do.   60

But they pulled me out of the sack,
And they stuck me together with glue.
And then I knew what to do.
I made a model of you,
A man in black with a Meinkampf look   65

And a love of the rack and the screw.
And I said I do, I do.
So daddy, I'm finally through.
The black telephone's off at the root,
The voices just can't worm through.   70

If I've killed one man, I've killed two—
The vampire who said he was you
And drank my blood for a year,
Seven years, if you want to know.
Daddy, you can lie back now.   75

There's a stake in your fat black heart
And the villagers never liked you.
They are dancing and stamping on you.
They always *knew* it was you.
Daddy, daddy, you bastard, I'm through.   80

152. The poem is based on the literary device of
    (A) coordinated juxtapositions
    (B) parallel vignettes
    (C) a central contradiction
    (D) a prolonged apostrophe
    (E) an extended metaphor

153. Referring to her father as "black shoe" (line 2) is an example of
    (A) metonymy
    (B) zeugma
    (C) caesura
    (D) appositive
    (E) simile

154. The predominant tone of the poem is one of
    (A) playful defiance
    (B) smoldering rage
    (C) bemused bitterness
    (D) ironic disengagement
    (E) angst-driven diffidence

155. In the second stanza, the imagery is primarily
    (A) reverential
    (B) hyperbolic
    (C) grotesque
    (D) ironic
    (E) oxymoronic

156. The eighth stanza (lines 36–40) is emblematic of the rest of the poem in its concern about
    (A) ruined cultural treasures
    (B) unsolved mysteries
    (C) bizarre forms of leisure
    (D) ethnic purity
    (E) magical thinking

157. Stanzas nine and ten (lines 41–50) include all of the following EXCEPT
    (A) apostrophe
    (B) synesthesia
    (C) irony
    (D) assonance
    (E) allusion

158. The ninth stanza (lines 41-45) includes
    (A) iambic rhythm
    (B) internal rhyme
    (C) assonance
    (D) synesthesia
    (E) cacophony

159. Stanzas eleven and twelve (lines 51–60) employ the poetic device of
    (A) iambic pentameter
    (B) literary conceit
    (C) octave
    (D) onomatopoeia
    (E) enjambment

160. There is a turning point in the narrator's mood in stanza
    (A) 9
    (B) 11
    (C) 13
    (D) 15
    (E) 16

161. Line 64, "I made a model of you," most closely means that the narrator
    (A) conceived a child
    (B) produced a photo or other image
    (C) constructed a voodoo doll
    (D) married a man like her father
    (E) projected aspects of her father on others

162. The final stanza serves primarily to
    (A) sum up the themes of the poem
    (B) extend an analogy from the previous stanza
    (C) expound on universal cultural themes
    (D) confirm the narrator's sense of despair
    (E) broaden the poem's thesis to a wider significance

163. The overall theme of the poem could be expressed as the narrator's
    (A) recognition of Oedipal urges
    (B) sense of the universality of familial conflicts
    (C) reaction to the horrors of Nazi Germany
    (D) profound confusion over her ethnic heritage
    (E) incapacitation by confused feelings about her father

See page 131 for the answers to this set of questions.

READING 13: "ARS POETICA" BY ARCHIBALD MACLEISH

QUESTIONS 164–177. Carefully read the poem before choosing your answers.

A poem should be palpable and mute
As a globed fruit,

Dumb
As old medallions to the thumb,

Silent as the sleeve-worn stone   5
Of casement ledges where the moss has grown—

A poem should be wordless
As the flight of birds.

*

A poem should be motionless in time
As the moon climbs,   10

Leaving, as the moon releases
Twig by twig the night-entangled trees,

Leaving, as the moon behind the winter leaves,
Memory by memory the mind—

A poem should be motionless in time   15
As the moon climbs.

*

A poem should be equal to:
Not true.

For all the history of grief
An empty doorway and a maple leaf.   20

For love
The leaning grasses and two lights above the sea—

A poem should not mean
But be.

164. The first two lines are an example of
(A) metaphor
(B) simile
(C) hamartia
(D) onomatopoeia
(E) trochee

165. "Dumb / As old medallions to the thumb" (lines 3–4) refers to
(A) a fruit
(B) palpability
(C) a poem
(D) muteness
(E) a poet

166. "Silent as the sleeve-worn stone / Of casement ledges where the moss has grown" (lines 5–6) is an example of
(A) alliteration
(B) metaphor
(C) personification
(D) hyperbole
(E) rhyme

167. "A poem should be wordless / As the flight of birds" (lines 7–8) suggests
(A) genre
(B) catharsis
(C) elision
(D) verbal irony
(E) hubris

168. "A poem should be motionless in time / As the moon climbs, / Leaving, as the moon releases / Twig by twig the night-entangled trees" (lines 9–12) shows
(A) a major image with loosely related sub-images
(B) unrelated images
(C) a series of sound images
(D) a series of touch images
(E) no images at all

169. "A poem should be equal to: / Not true" (lines 17–18) reflects
(A) the scientific aspects of poetry
(B) the mathematical aspects of poetry
(C) the relationship of poetry to life's inconsistencies
(D) the astronomical aspects of poetry
(E) the perfection expected of poetry

170. The major images in the poem suggest
(A) hope
(B) a paradox
(C) decay
(D) anger
(E) delight

171. "For all the history of grief / An empty doorway and a maple leaf" (lines 19–20) tells a brief poetic story that suggests
(A) loss and gloom replaced by cheer
(B) a happy tale
(C) a sad tale
(D) a philosophical tale
(E) a religious tale

172. "For love / The leaning grasses and two lights above the sea"
(lines 21–22) may refer to
(A) the grass
(B) the sun and the moon
(C) two lovers forever kept apart
(D) a love of philosophy
(E) both (B) and (C)

173. The words "A poem should be" are used repeatedly and are
examples of
(A) metaphor
(B) simile
(C) anaphora
(D) terza rima
(E) villanelle

174. The opening images of the poem stress
(A) the paradoxical
(B) the time
(C) the tangible
(D) the philosophical
(E) happiness

175. "Memory by memory the mind" (line 14) is an example of
(A) sprung rhythm
(B) alliteration
(C) ottava rima
(D) rhyme royal
(E) elision

176. According to MacLeish, "A poem should not mean / But be"
(lines 23–24) is the essence of
(A) life
(B) poetry
(C) Elizabethan poetry
(D) classical poetry
(E) religion

177. The entire poem
(A) does exactly what the author says poetry should not do
(B) does what the author says poetry should do
(C) shows an easy analysis of poetry
(D) shows the clear story of life
(E) shows the emptiness of life

See page 131 for the answers to this set of questions.

READING 14: "TO THE VIRGINS, TO MAKE MUCH OF TIME" BY ROBERT HERRICK

QUESTIONS 178–188. Carefully read the poem before choosing your answers.

Gather ye rosebuds while ye may,
    Old Time is still a-flying;
And this same flower that smiles today
    Tomorrow will be dying.

The glorious lamp of heaven, the Sun,   5
    The higher he's a-getting,
The sooner will his race be run,
    And nearer he's to setting.

That age is best which is the first,
    When youth and blood are warmer;   10
But being spent, the worse, and worst
    Times still succeed the former.

Then be not coy, but use your time;
    And while ye may, go marry;
For having lost but once your prime,   15
    You may forever tarry.

178. The poem is a
    (A) ballad
    (B) narrative poem
    (C) paean
    (D) lyric poem
    (E) limerick

179. The meter form alternates between
    (A) tetrameter and trimeter
    (B) monometer and nonometer
    (C) pentameter and heptameter
    (D) hexameter and octometer
    (E) dimeter and pentameter

180. The poem includes all of the following EXCEPT
    (A) antithesis
    (B) personification
    (C) slant rhyme
    (D) an appositive
    (E) alliteration

181. In the phrase "Gather ye" (line 1), "ye" most closely means
    (A) the intimate form of "you"
    (B) the imperative "you"
    (C) you who are gathered here
    (D) your
    (E) yes

182. The four stanzas of the poem include
    (A) three allusions and a metaphor
    (B) three examples and a concession
    (C) four metaphorical conceits
    (D) three analogies and an admonition
    (E) three parallel situations and one anomaly

183. The point of the second stanza is that
    (A) time is passing quickly
    (B) it's almost midsummer
    (C) the sun is losing its power
    (D) life is glorious
    (E) the heavens approve of love

184. The point of the third stanza is that
    (A) old age brings wisdom as well as sorrow
    (B) even the worst of times shall pass
    (C) youth's passions run too hot
    (D) life grows more difficult with time
    (E) with time and patience comes success

185. The word "may" in the fourth stanza (line 14) most closely means
    (A) are still attractive enough to
    (B) have permission to
    (C) have the will to
    (D) can abide to
    (E) desire to

186. The phrase "having lost but once your prime" (line 15) most closely means having
    (A) lost the capacity for love
    (B) lost one's athletic ability
    (C) become less attractive
    (D) attained legal age
    (E) reached the age of innocence

187. The tone of the poem is
    (A) ominous
    (B) amorous
    (C) derisive
    (D) funereal
    (E) sportive

188. The lines that most closely echo the title are
    I. lines 1–2
    II. lines 5–6
    III. lines 13–14
    IV. lines 15–16
    (A) I and II only
    (B) I, II, and III only
    (C) II, III, and IV only
    (D) IV only
    (E) I, II, III, and IV

See page 132 for the answers to this set of questions.

READING 15: EXCERPT FROM *DEATH OF A SALESMAN* BY ARTHUR MILLER

QUESTIONS 189–203. Carefully read the passage, the conclusion of the play, before choosing your answers.

> . . . *All stare down at the grave.*

REQUIEM

CHARLEY: It's getting dark, Linda.

Linda doesn't react. She stares at the grave.

BIFF: How about it, Mom? Better get some rest, heh?
They'll be closing the gate soon.   5

Linda makes no move. Pause.

HAPPY: (*deeply angered*) He had no right to do that! There
was no necessity for it. We would've helped him.

CHARLEY: (*grunting*) Hmmm.

BIFF: Come along, Mom.   10

LINDA: Why didn't anybody come?

CHARLEY: It was a very nice funeral.

LINDA: But where are all the people he knew? Maybe they
blame him.

CHARLEY: Naa. It's a rough world, Linda. They wouldn't   15
blame him.

LINDA: I can't understand it. At this time especially. First
time in thirty-five years we were just about free and
clear. He only needed a little salary. He was even
finished with the dentist.   20

CHARLEY: No man only needs a little salary.

LINDA: I can't understand it.

BIFF: There were a lot of nice days. When he'd come home
from a trip; or on Sundays, making the stoop; finishing
the cellar; putting on the new porch; when he built the   25
extra bathroom; and put up the garage. You know
something, Charley, there's more of him in that front
stoop than in all the sales he ever made.

CHARLEY: Yeah. He was a happy man with a batch of
cement.   30

LINDA: He was so wonderful with his hands.

BIFF: He had the wrong dreams. All, all, wrong.

HAPPY: (*almost ready to fight Biff*) Don't say that!

BIFF: He never knew who he was.

CHARLEY: (*stopping Happy's movement and reply. To Biff.*)   35
Nobody dast blame this man. You don't understand:
Willy was a salesman. And for a salesman, there is no
rock bottom to the life. He don't put a bolt to a nut, he
don't tell you the law or give you medicine. He's a man
out there in the blue, riding on a smile and a shoeshine.   40
And when they start not smiling back—that's an
earthquake. And then you get yourself a couple of spots
on your hat, and you're finished. Nobody dast blame
this man. A salesman is got to dream, boy. It comes
with the territory.   45

BIFF: Charley, the man didn't know who he was.

HAPPY: (*infuriated*) Don't say that!

BIFF: Why don't you come with me, Happy?

HAPPY: I'm not licked that easily. I'm staying right in this city, and I'm gonna beat this racket! (*He looks at Biff, his chin set.*) The Loman Brothers! 50

BIFF: I know who I am, kid.

HAPPY: All right, boy. I'm gonna show you and everybody else that Willy Loman did not die in vain. He had a good dream. It's the only dream you can have—to come out number-one man. He fought it out here, and this is where I'm gonna win it for him. 55

BIFF: (*with a hopeless glance at Happy, bends toward his mother*) Let's go, Mom.

LINDA: I'll be with you in a minute. Go on, Charley. (*He hesitates.*) I want to, just for a minute. I never had a chance to say good-by. 60

Charley moves away, followed by Happy. Biff remains a slight distance up and left of Linda. She sits there, summoning herself. The flute begins, not far away, playing behind her speech. 65

LINDA: Forgive me, dear. I can't cry. I don't know what it is, but I can't cry. I don't understand it. Why did you ever do that? Help me, Willy, I can't cry. It seems to me that you're just on another trip. I keep expecting you. Willy, dear, I can't cry. Why did you do it? I search and search and I search, and I can't understand it, Willy. I made the last payment on the house today. Today, dear. And there'll be nobody home. (*A sob rises in her throat.*) We're free and clear. (*Sobbing more fully, released.*) We're free. (*Biff comes slowly toward her.*) We're free . . . We're free . . . 70 75

Biff lifts her to her feet and moves out up right with her in his arms. Linda sobs quietly. Bernard and Charley come together and follow them, followed by Happy. Only the music of the flute is left on the darkening stage as over the house the hard towers of the apartment buildings rise into sharp focus, and— 80

The Curtain Falls

189. When Linda says, "I can't understand it. At this time especially. First time in thirty-five years we were just about free and clear. He only needed a little salary. He was even finished with the dentist" (lines 17–20), her words are filled with

(A) irony

(B) sadness

(C) empathy

(D) irony, empathy, and sadness

(E) irony and sadness

190. Happy angrily says, "He had no right to do that! There was no necessity for it. We would've helped him" (lines 7–8); the words "that" and "it" refer to
    (A) Willy's death
    (B) the involuntary dying
    (C) the accidental death
    (D) the loss of Willy's job
    (E) the loss of Willy's credibility

191. The word "dast," used twice by Charley (lines 36 and 43), means
    (A) chortle
    (B) drone
    (C) dare
    (D) ponder
    (E) laugh

192. Biff says, "There were a lot of nice days. . . . You know something, Charley, there's more of him in that front stoop than in all the sales he ever made" (lines 23–28). This is a vivid example of
    I. the realization of the American dream
    II. the undiscovered waste of a life
    III. the love of a wife and children
    (A) I and II only
    (B) I, II, and III
    (C) III only
    (D) II only
    (E) I and III only

193. Charley says, "He's a man out there in the blue, riding on a smile and a shoeshine. And when they start not smiling back—that's an earthquake" (lines 39–42). The sentiment of these words
    (A) tugs at the audience's heartstrings
    (B) shows a cool, indifferent statement of fact
    (C) describes hatred for family
    (D) shows hatred
    (E) shows fear

194. In lines 32–34, the dialogue between Biff and Happy shows
    (A) filial love examined and rectified
    (B) anguish, betrayal, and candor
    (C) a lack of dreaming and scrutiny
    (D) a keen sense of business acumen
    (E) paternal love ridiculed

195. In "A salesman is got to dream, boy. It comes with the territory" (lines 44–45), the phrase "comes with the territory" is
    (A) standard technical parlance
    (B) a law of business
    (C) idiomatic
    (D) a legal term
    (E) hyperbole

196. "First time in thirty-five years we were just about free and clear. He only needed a little salary. He was even finished with the dentist" (lines 17–20) shows
(A) Willy earned a large salary
(B) Willy was destitute
(C) Willy was heroic
(D) the dental plan was in effect
(E) the American dream backfired

197. In lines 29–30, Charley says, "Yeah. He was a happy man with a batch of cement." With respect to someone in Willy's chosen profession, such a comment is
(A) emblematic
(B) incongruous
(C) socialistic
(D) unstable
(E) pedantic

198. In line 40, Charley uses the phrase "riding on a smile and a shoeshine." Even thought this is a prose drama, here the playwright is using a poetic device known as
(A) caesura
(B) simile
(C) hyperbole
(D) reification
(E) invocation

199. In lines 53–54, Happy says, "All right, boy. I'm gonna show you and everybody else that Willy Loman did not die in vain," indicating
(A) that not one person in Willy's family or place of employment ever really loved him
(B) that only Linda really understood Willy
(C) Happy's pride and continuing refusal to accept the harsh reality
(D) that Willy did actually die in vain
(E) that Willy did finally achieve all his goals in life

200. In the scene direction in line 65, the words "summoning herself" refer to Linda's
(A) dispirited outcry
(B) happy thoughts of the past
(C) self-hypnotic thoughts on the denial of family memories
(D) lingering thoughts of her hatred of Willy
(E) futile attempts at real sorrow

201. Arthur Miller purposefully termed the entire last section of the play a requiem. With respect to the word "requiem," all of the following statements are true EXCEPT which one?
(A) The American dream is now dead.
(B) The dreams of the family left behind now seem dead.
(C) There is a new and reliable hope for the future that builds on Willy's remarkable business successes in the past.
(D) The era of the traveling salesman is dead.
(E) Willy's way of life is now dead.

202. In lines 24 and 28, the word "stoop" acts grammatically as a
    (A) verb
    (B) adjective
    (C) noun
    (D) adverb
    (E) preposition

203. The haunting sound of the flute is an integral part of this section
    of Miller's play because it
    (A) provides the sound effect to his crashing entrance into the
        afterlife
    (B) is symbolic of Willy's futile pursuit of the American Dream
    (C) is reminiscent of Willy's funeral service
    (D) is symbolic of his successful life
    (E) will become Biff and Happy's theme song of a bright future

See page 132 for the answers to this set of questions.

READING 16: "MAIN CHARACTER"
BY JIMMY SANTIAGO BACA

QUESTIONS 204–216. Carefully read the poem before choosing your answers.

> I went to see
> *How the West Was Won*
> at the Sunshine Theater.
> Five years old,
> deep in a plush seat,   5
> light turned off,
> bright screen lit up
> with MGM roaring lion—
>   in front of me
>   a drunk Indian rose,   10
>   cursed
>   the western violins
>   and hurled his uncapped bagged bottle
>   of wine
>   at the rocket roaring to the moon.   15
> His dark angry body
> convulsed with his obscene gestures
> at the screen,
> and then ushers escorted him
> up the aisle,   20
> and as he staggered past me,
> I heard his grieving sobs.
>   Red wine streaked
>   blue sky and take-off smoke,
>   sizzled cowboys' campfires,   25
>   dripped down barbwire,
>   slogged the brave, daring scouts
>   who galloped off to mesa buttes
>   to speak peace with Apaches,
>   and made the prairie   30
>   lush with wine streams.
> When the movie
> was over,
> I squinted at the bright
> sunny street outside,   35
> looking for the main character.

204. The typography of the poem
    (A) symbolizes opposition between the narrator and the Indian
    (B) creates stanzas
    (C) heightens the contrast between film and reality
    (D) underscores an opposition between setting and action
    (E) instills a sense of dizziness

205. The tone of the poem overall is
    (A) detached
    (B) sad
    (C) puzzled
    (D) angry
    (E) inquisitive

206. The power of lines 9–15 resides in
    (A) the intensity of the image
    (B) the narrator's obvious sympathy for the Indian
    (C) confusion over whether the Indian is in the film
    (D) connotations of freedom and imprisonment
    (E) stark contrasts between old and new

207. Lines 9–15 include all of the following EXCEPT
    (A) alliteration
    (B) a full sentence
    (C) assonance
    (D) a compound verb
    (E) personification

208. The "wine" in lines 22–31
    (A) refers to the Eucharist
    (B) symbolizes Western domination
    (C) refers to the Indian's level of intoxication
    (D) symbolizes the effect the Indian has had on the narrator
    (E) provides a reason for the narrator's confusion

209. Lines 23–31 include all of the following EXCEPT
    (A) enjambment
    (B) elision
    (C) alliteration
    (D) double entendre
    (E) onomatopoeia

210. The rhyme scheme of lines 23–31 is primarily
    (A) slant
    (B) feminine
    (C) masculine
    (D) internal
    (E) nonexistent

211. The poem relates a
    (A) rite of passage
    (B) parallel universe
    (C) loss of innocence
    (D) moment of shared understanding
    (E) betrayal

212. The poet portrays the Indian as
    (A) reprehensible
    (B) pitiable
    (C) laudable
    (D) heroic
    (E) vindicated

213. The poem moves from
    (A) resentment to acceptance
    (B) premise to conclusion
    (C) light to dark
    (D) cause to effect
    (E) hope to despair

214. The last lines (32–36)
    (A) offer a summing up
    (B) present an alternative interpretation
    (C) shift to a new point of view
    (D) broaden the theme to a universal level
    (E) add irony to lines 1 and 2

215. The second indented section of the poem provides
    (A) a precise description of the film
    (B) a prescient vision of the future
    (C) silver screen images distorted by imagination
    (D) moments of profound epiphany
    (E) personal reflection and meditation

216. Based on a reading of this poem, one can surmise that the poet
    (A) is an Indian
    (B) admires traditional ways
    (C) resents Western ideology
    (D) believes that conquest has far-reaching effects
    (E) wants to offer retribution to Indians

See page 132 for the answers to this set of questions.

READING 17: EXCERPT FROM *OEDIPUS REX* BY SOPHOCLES

QUESTIONS 217–226. Carefully read the passage, the conclusion of the play, before choosing your answers.

<pre>
OEDIPUS: . . . Children, where are you?
        Come quickly to my hands: they are your brother's—
        Hands that have brought your father's once clear eyes
        To this way of seeing—
                        Ah dearest ones,   5
        I had neither sight nor knowledge then, your father
        By the woman who was the source of his own life!
        And I weep for you—having no strength to see you—
        I weep for you when I think of the bitterness
        That men will visit upon you all your lives.   10
        What homes, what festivals can you attend
        Without being forced to depart again in tears?
        And when you come to marriageable age,
        Where is the man, my daughters, who would dare
        Risk the bane that lies on all my children?   15
        Is there any evil wanting? Your father killed
        His father; sowed the womb of her who bore him;
        Engendered you at the fount of his own existence!
        That is what they will say of you.
                        Then, whom   20
        Can you ever marry? There are no bridegrooms for you,
        And your lives must wither away in sterile dreaming.
        O Kreon, son of Menoikeus!
        You are the only father my daughters have,
        Since we, their parents, are both of us gone for ever. 25
        They are your own blood: you will not let them
        Fall into beggary and loneliness;
        You will keep them from the miseries that are mine!
        Take pity on them; see, they are only children,
        Friendless except for you. Promise me this,   30
        Great prince, and give me your hand in token of it.
        (Kreon clasps his right hand.)
        Children:
        I could say much, if you could understand me,
        But as it is, I have only this prayer for you: 35
        Live where you can, be as happy as you can—
        Happier, please God, than God has made your father.
</pre>

217. In telling his daughters, "I had neither sight not knowledge then, your father / By the woman who was the source of his own life!" (lines 6–7), Oedipus means that
    I. he did not know he was their brother
    II. he did not know their mother was his mother
    III. he was their father
    (A) I and II only
    (B) II and III only
    (C) I, II, and III
    (D) I only
    (E) II only

218. In ". . . the bitterness / That men will visit upon you all your lives" (lines 9–10), "visit upon you" means
    (A) forgive you
    (B) thrust upon you
    (C) force you to make a journey
    (D) send you on a sacred pilgrimage
    (E) kill you

219. In "Risk the bane that lies on my children?" (line 15), the word "bane" means
    (A) trouble
    (B) death
    (C) running
    (D) laughing
    (E) cheering

220. "Your father killed / His father; sowed the womb of her who bore him; / Engendered you at the fount of his own existence!" (lines 16–17) refers to
    (A) fratricide and marriage
    (B) regicide and matricide
    (C) intended patricide
    (D) unintended patricide
    (E) premeditated murder

221. In "Is there any evil wanting?" (line 16), the word "wanting" means
    (A) hoping
    (B) lacking
    (C) needing
    (D) filling
    (E) describing

222. Line 17, "sowed the womb of her who bore him," is a metaphoric way of describing the fact that Oedipus
    (A) had sexual relations with his mother
    (B) had farmers who worked for him
    (C) had two mothers
    (D) was naïve
    (E) was an exceptional gardener

223. In the lines "you will not let them / Fall into beggary and
     loneliness" (26–27), the "you" refers to
     (A) Oedipus
     (B) Kreon
     (C) Menoikeus
     (D) the father of Oedipus
     (E) the mother of Oedipus

224. In "There are no bridegrooms for you, / And your lives must
     wither away in sterile dreaming," (lines 21–22) the word "sterile"
     gives a vision of a(n)
     (A) austere future
     (B) refreshing past
     (C) crafty reconcilement
     (D) legal conundrum
     (E) after-thought of great expectation

225. "Children, where are you? / Come quickly to my hands: they are
     your brother's— /" (lines 1–2) emphasizes
     (A) the strange father-and-sibling relationship
     (B) the normal mother-and-daughter relationship
     (C) a definite lack of fatalism
     (D) the essence of hope
     (E) the misguided but happy fortune of Oedipus

226. Lines 36–37, "be as happy as you can— / Happier, please God,
     than God has made your father," suggest
     (A) their fate is sealed and there will be no hope
     (B) there may be hope that a father's prayer will be answered
     (C) their fate shows that Kreon will kill them
     (D) their fate shows that Oedipus will ask his wife for help
     (E) there is no such a thing as fate in a Greek play

See page 132 for the answers to this set of questions.

READING 18: EXCERPT FROM "CATHEDRAL" BY RAYMOND CARVER

QUESTIONS 227–236. Carefully read the passage, from near the end of the story, before choosing your answers. The story describes the narrator's discomfort when his wife invites a friend from before their marriage, a blind man, to their home for dinner. Now it is late, and only he and the blind man are still awake, sitting in front of the television.

"Cathedrals," the blind man said. He sat up and rolled his head back and forth. "If you want the truth, bub, that's about all I know. What I just said. What I heard him say. But maybe you could describe one to me? I wish you'd do it. I'd like that. If you want to know, I really don't have a good idea." 5

I stared hard at the shot of the cathedral on the TV. How could I even begin to describe it? But say my life depended on it. Say my life was being threatened by an insane guy who said I had to do it or else.

I stared some more at the cathedral before the picture 10 flipped off into the countryside. There was no use. I turned to the blind man and said, "To begin with, they're very tall." I was looking around the room for clues. "They reach way up. Up and up. Toward the sky. They're so big, some of them, they have to have these supports. To help hold them up, so to 15 speak. These supports are called buttresses. They remind me of viaducts,[1] for some reason. But maybe you don't know viaducts, either? Sometimes the cathedrals have devils and such carved into the front. Sometimes lords and ladies. Don't ask me why this is," I said. 20

He was nodding. The whole upper part of his body seemed to be moving back and forth.

"I'm not doing so good, am I?" I said.

He stopped nodding and leaned forward on the edge of the sofa. As he listened to me, he was running his fingers 25 through his beard. I wasn't getting through to him, I could see that. But he waited for me to go on just the same. He nodded, like he was trying to encourage me. I tried to think what else to say. "They're really big," I said. "They're massive. They're built of stone. Marble, too, sometimes. In 30 those olden days, when they built cathedrals, men wanted to be close to God. In those olden days, God was an important part of everyone's life. You could tell this from their cathedral-building. I'm sorry," I said, "but it looks like that's the best I can do for you. I'm just no good at it." 35

"That's all right, bub," the blind man said. "Hey, listen. I hope you don't mind my asking you. Can I ask you something? Let me ask you a simple question, yes or no. I'm just curious and there's no offense. You're my host. But let me ask if you are in any way religious? You don't mind my 40 asking?"

---

[1] Long, elevated roadways.

I shook my head. He couldn't see that, though. A wink is the same as a nod to a blind man. "I guess I don't believe in it. In anything. Sometimes it's hard. You know what I'm saying?" 45

"Sure, I do," he said.

"Right," I said.

The Englishman [on the television] was still holding forth. My wife sighed in her sleep. She drew a long breath and went on with her sleeping. 50

"You'll have to forgive me," I said. "But I can't tell you what a cathedral looks like. It just isn't in me to do it. I can't do any more than I've done."

The blind man sat very still, his head down, as he listened to me. 55

I said, "The truth is, cathedrals don't mean anything special to me. Nothing. Cathedrals. They're something to look at on late-night TV. That's all they are."

It was then that the blind man cleared his throat. He brought something up. He took a handkerchief from his back pocket. Then he said, "I get it, bub. It's okay. It happens. Don't worry about it," he said. "Hey, listen to me. Will you do me a favor? I got an idea. Why don't you find us some heavy paper? And a pen. We'll do something. We'll draw one together. Get us a pen and some heavy paper. Go on, bub, get the stuff," he said. 60

65

So I went upstairs. My legs felt like they didn't have any strength in them. They felt like they did after I'd done some running. In my wife's room, I looked around. I found some ballpoints in a little basket on her table. And then I tried to think where to look for the kind of paper he was talking about. 70

Downstairs, in the kitchen, I found a shopping bag with onion skins in the bottom of the bag. I emptied the bag and shook it. I brought it into the living room and sat down with it near his legs. 75

I moved some things, smoothed the wrinkles from the bag, spread it out on the coffee table.

The blind man got down from the sofa and sat next to me on the carpet. 80

He ran his fingers over the paper. He went up and down the sides of the paper. The edges, even the edges. He fingered the corners.

"All right," he said. "All right, let's do her."

He found my hand, the hand with the pen. He closed his hand over my hand. "Go ahead, bub, draw," he said. "Draw. You'll see. I'll follow along with you. It'll be okay. Just begin now like I'm telling you. You'll see. Draw," the blind man said. 85

So I began. First I drew a box that looked like a house. It could have been the house I lived in. Then I put a roof on it. At either end of the roof, I drew spires. Crazy. 90

"Swell," he said. "Terrific. You're doing fine," he said. "Never thought anything like this could happen in your lifetime, did you, bub? Well, it's a strange life, we all know that. Go on now. Keep it up." 95

I put in windows with arches. I drew flying buttresses. I hung great doors. I couldn't stop. The TV station went off the air. I put down the pen and closed and opened my fingers. The blind man felt around over the paper. He moved the tips 100 of his fingers over the paper, all over what I had drawn, and he nodded.

"Doing fine," the blind man said.

I took up the pen again, and he found my hand. I kept at it. I'm no artist. But I kept drawing just the same. 105

227. In this excerpt, the author relies primarily on which of the following to convey emotion?
(A) the mood of the setting
(B) charged language
(C) symbolism
(D) description of gestures
(E) dialogue

228. At the end of this excerpt the narrator is most surprised at
(A) his own enthusiasm
(B) his ability to draw
(C) the blind man's impertinence
(D) the blind man's curiosity
(E) the beauty of cathedrals

229. Carver chose cathedrals as the prominent motif of his story because
(A) they are relatively easy to draw
(B) of their historical significance
(C) they represent humankind's hubris
(D) they are massive and solid, yet beautiful
(E) they signify humankind's spiritual longing

230. When the blind man asks if the narrator is "in any way religious" (line 40), the narrator
(A) doesn't answer truthfully
(B) at first evades the question, then offers a partial answer
(C) answers honestly and openly
(D) realizes that he actually is religious
(E) is too shy to convey his real religious sentiments

231. What is the thematic significance of the dinner guest being's blind?
(A) It symbolizes a life lived without meaning.
(B) His physical blindness mirrors the narrator's spiritual blindness.
(C) It demonstrates the narrator's open-mindedness.
(D) It makes him less threatening as a former rival for his wife.
(E) It alludes to a blind prophet in Greek mythology.

232. In the context of the passage, the characters' watching a
     television show on cathedrals can be seen as
     (A) blasphemous
     (B) educational
     (C) symbolic
     (D) spiritually uplifting
     (E) prodigal

233. The pace of the narrative can be described as
     (A) stately
     (B) plodding
     (C) brisk
     (D) deliberate
     (E) erratic

234. The passage "I put in windows with arches. I drew flying
     buttresses. I hung great doors. I couldn't stop" (lines 97–98)
     exemplifies the
     (A) progressive synecdoche
     (B) use of zeugma
     (C) ironic motif
     (D) anaphora
     (E) periodic sentence

235. The statement "Never thought anything like this could happen in
     your lifetime, did you, bub?" (lines 93–94) is an example of
     (A) hyperbole
     (B) a double entendre
     (C) an oxymoron
     (D) comic seriousness
     (E) a satirical aside

236. The tone of the passage is
     (A) ironic
     (B) satiric
     (C) insistent
     (D) maudlin
     (E) frank

See page 132 for the answers to this set of questions.

READING 19: "KUBLA KHAN, OR, A VISION IN A DREAM. A FRAGMENT" BY SAMUEL TAYLOR COLERIDGE

QUESTIONS 237–249. Carefully read the poem before choosing your answers.

In Xanadu did Kubla Khan
A stately pleasure-dome decree:
Where Alph, the sacred river, ran
Through caverns measureless to man
Down to a sunless sea.   5
So twice five miles of fertile ground
With walls and towers were girdled round;
And there were gardens bright with sinuous rills,
Where blossomed many an incense-bearing tree;
And here were forests ancient as the hills,   10
Enfolding sunny spots of greenery.

But oh! that deep romantic chasm which slanted
Down the green hill athwart a cedarn cover!
A savage place! as holy and enchanted
As e'er beneath a waning moon was haunted   15
By woman wailing for her demon-lover!
And from this chasm, with ceaseless turmoil seething,
As if this earth in fast thick pants were breathing,
A mighty fountain momently was forced:
Amid whose swift half-intermitted burst   20
Huge fragments vaulted like rebounding hail,
Or chaffy grain beneath the thresher's flail:
And 'mid these dancing rocks at once and ever
It flung up momently the sacred river.
Five miles meandering with a mazy motion   25
Through wood and dale the sacred river ran,
Then reached the caverns measureless to man,
And sank in tumult to a lifeless ocean:
And 'mid this tumult Kubla heard from far
Ancestral voices prophesying war!   30

The shadow of the dome of pleasure
Floated midway on the waves;
Where was heard the mingled measure
From the fountain and the caves.
It was a miracle of rare device,   35
A sunny pleasure-dome with caves of ice!

A damsel with a dulcimer
In a vision once I saw:
It was an Abyssinian maid,
And on her dulcimer she played,   40
Singing of Mount Abora.
Could I revive within me
Her symphony and song,

       To such a deep delight 'twould win me,
       That with music loud and long,   45
       I would build that dome in air,
       That sunny dome! those caves of ice!
       And all who heard should see them there,
       And all should cry, Beware! Beware!   50
       His flashing eyes, his floating hair!
       Weave a circle round him thrice,
       And close your eyes with holy dread,
       For he on honey-dew hath fed,
       And drunk the milk of Paradise.

237. The atmosphere in lines 1–5 is
    (A) obscure
    (B) resplendent
    (C) clear yet mysterious
    (D) falsifying
    (E) nostalgic

238. The term "pleasure-dome" (line 2) refers to
    I. an assembled corporeal structure
    II. a monument that symbolizes imagination
    III. the uncorrupted creation of invention
    (A) I only
    (B) II only
    (C) I and II only
    (D) I, II, and III
    (E) III only

239. In line 8, "rills" refers to each of the following EXCEPT
    (A) riparian areas
    (B) streams
    (C) creeks
    (D) rivulets
    (E) runs

240. In line 29, "tumult" means
    I. pandemonium and bedlam
    II. a state of complete euphoria
    III. amity, concord, and civility
    (A) I and III only
    (B) I only
    (C) II only
    (D) III only
    (E) II and III only

241. The main theme of the poem is the
    (A) results of mutual respect for weather and ego
    (B) results of breaking the eternal rules by creating heaven on
        earth
    (C) results of a hermit's reclusiveness and ascetic life
    (D) pleasingly good-natured event
    (E) absence of iniquity

242. In line 39, "It" refers to
    (A) the damsel
    (B) the maid
    (C) the dulcimer
    (D) both (B) and (C)
    (E) both (A) and (B)

243. In line 18, "pants" is a(n)
    (A) noun and object of the preposition "in"
    (B) verb and predicate of the entire sentence
    (C) noun meaning clothing
    (D) adjective modifying the word "breathing"
    (E) gerund used as the subject of a clause

244. The entire poem contrasts
    (A) a man-made utopia and a doomed annihilation
    (B) the building of an earthly paradise and the inability to defy
        diabolical forces
    (C) a positive vision and a negative insidious power
    (D) war and peace
    (E) affection and abhorrence

245. The images of the hail (line 21) and the grain (line 22) represent
    (A) the music of the caves
    (B) the water from the mighty fountain
    (C) the sound of the dulcimer
    (D) the rocks
    (E) the wailing for the demon-lover

246. In line 13, "athwart" means
    (A) no movement at all
    (B) in the direction of
    (C) movement from one side to the other
    (D) guile amid hope
    (E) faithful leanings

247. In lines 50–53, the words "he" and "his" refer specifically to
    (A) the personification of measureless caverns
    (B) Kubla Khan himself
    (C) the physical embodiment of the sacred rivers
    (D) the poet
    (E) the unnamed narrator

248. The individual character who awakens the desire to build the
    pleasure-dome in air is
    (A) Kubla Khan
    (B) the demon-lover
    (C) Alph
    (D) the Abyssinian maid
    (E) Xanadu

249. Taken in its entirety, the psychological interpretation of the actual landscape described in the poem suggests
    (A) the sensual and sense-evoking surface covering that represents a dull mind
    (B) the subterranean landscape that represents nothingness
    (C) the exclusivity of the conscious rational mind
    (D) a true dichotomy between the sensual and the rational aspects present in both life and the poem
    (E) utopian dreams fulfilled willy-nilly

See page 132 for the answers to this set of questions.

READING 20: "THE PLOT" BY JORGE LUIS BORGES

QUESTIONS 250–259. Carefully read this complete short story before choosing your answers.

> To make his horror perfect, Caesar,[1] hemmed about at the foot of a statue by his friends' impatient knives, discovers among the faces and the blades the face of Marcus Junius Brutus,[2] his ward, perhaps his very son—and so Caesar stops defending himself, and cries out *Et tu, Brute?*[3] Shakespeare and Quevedo[4] record that pathetic cry. 5
>
> Fate is partial to repetitions, variations, symmetries. Nineteen centuries later, in the southern part of the province of Buenos Aires, a gaucho[5] is set 10 upon by other gauchos, and as he falls he recognizes a godson of his, and says to him in gentle remonstrance and slow surprise (these words must be heard, not read): *Pero, che!*[6] He dies, but he does not know that he has died so that a scene can be played out again. 15

250. Lines 1–2 include a
(A) synesthesia
(B) personification
(C) litotes
(D) soliloquy
(E) zeugma

251. Lines 4–5 include a(n)
(A) apostrophe
(B) appositive
(C) double entendre
(D) metaphor
(E) allusion

252. The sentence in lines 1–6 is a(n)
(A) periodic sentence
(B) aphorism
(C) interior monologue
(D) apostrophe
(E) satirical aside

---

[1]Julius Caesar (100 B.C.–44 B.C.), Roman dictator assassinated by a band of conspirators.
[2] Marcus Junius Brutus: Roman politician (85 B.C.–42 B.C.) and the lead conspirator who assassinated Julius Caesar.
[3] Latin for *You too, Brutus?*
[4] Francisco Gómez de Quevedo y Villegas (1580–1645), Spanish poet and satirist.
[5] South American cowboy.
[6]Spanish expression expressing surprise.

253. In contrast to the first paragraph, the second paragraph offers a(n)
    (A) antithesis
    (B) satirical version
    (C) lyrical digression
    (D) quotidian example
    (E) hyperbolic commentary

254. The most discordant word in the first paragraph is
    (A) "perfect" (line 1)
    (B) "impatient" (line 2)
    (C) "son" (line 5)
    (D) "stops" (line5)
    (E) "pathetic" (line 7)

255. Lines 13–14 include a(n)
    (A) stage direction
    (B) aphorism
    (C) satirical observation
    (D) literary conceit
    (E) authorial aside

256. The story serves primarily as a
    (A) parody of a canonical work of literature
    (B) reflection on the nature of stories
    (C) meditation on the cyclical nature of revenge
    (D) satire of conventional story structure
    (E) sentimentalized retelling of a classic story

257. The tone of the story is
    (A) diffident
    (B) ostentatious
    (C) austere
    (D) priggish
    (E) enigmatic

258. The reason Caesar and the gaucho stop defending themselves is that they
    (A) are outnumbered
    (B) feel vindicated
    (C) accept their fate
    (D) mistakenly think they are safe
    (E) hope for pity

259. The significance of the last sentence
    (A) relies on an ambiguity of the referent of "he"
    (B) demonstrates the futility of diplomacy
    (C) underscores the social significance of myth
    (D) indicates that the gauchos will set upon one another
    (E) disproves that revenge is cyclical

See page 132 for the answers to this set of questions.

READING 21: "HOW DO I LOVE THEE?" BY ELIZABETH BARRETT BROWNING

QUESTIONS 260–74. Carefully read the poem before choosing your answers.

How do I love thee? Let me count the ways.
I love thee to the depth and breadth and height
My soul can reach, when feeling out of sight
For the ends of being and ideal grace.
I love thee to the level of every day's   5
Most quiet need, by sun and candle-light.
I love thee freely, as men strive for right.
I love thee purely, as they turn from praise.
I love thee with the passion put to use
In my old griefs, and with my childhood's faith.   10
I love thee with a love I seemed to lose
With my lost saints. I love thee with the breath,
Smiles, tears, of all my life; and, if God choose,
I shall but love thee better after death.

260. The poem is an example of
(A) an Elizabethan sonnet
(B) an Italian sonnet
(C) an American paradox
(D) a French villanelle
(E) a Scottish pastoral romance

261. Lines 1–8 show
(A) no statement of the problem and no revelation on the means
   to solve it
(B) no answers to the many questions posed
(C) no similarity between the poet's love and her political
   principles
(D) a formulation exemplifying a similarity between the poet's
   love and her religious ideals
(E) help for dissolution of the love affair

262. The last six lines (lines 9–14) of the poem
(A) show the shallowness of her love
(B) indicate the passion of love she has not attained
(C) show that love is merely earthly
(D) express that she will love her husband-to-be even more after
   death
(E) indicate that too many questions are left unanswered

263. The poem is filled with
(A) examples of anaphora and alliteration
(B) free verse and lack of rhythm
(C) examples of hubris and personification
(D) portrayals of despair and desperation
(E) mundane portrayals of unattainable love

264. The question in line 1, "How do I love thee?" is a
    (A) literal question under the guise of the ostentatious
    (B) rhetorical question under the guise of the literal
    (C) pretentious question with no guise at all
    (D) contrived question under the guise of the conspicuous
    (E) literal question under the guise of the rhetorical

265. The overall tone of the poem shows love to be
    (A) fervent and boundless
    (B) unrestrained and fettered
    (C) unfettered and restrained
    (D) absent the poet
    (E) absent the poet's lover

266. "I love thee to the depth and breadth and height / My soul can reach" (lines 2–3) refers to the
    (A) wind, rain, and other precipitation the soul can reach
    (B) hope, skill, and determination the soul attaches to
    (C) total prominence, proportions, and undersurface the soul can grasp
    (D) lack of love after death
    (E) love that can and must be delegated

267. "I love thee" (line 2), intensified by "to the level" (line 5), "freely" (line 7), "purely" (line 8), "with the passion" (line 9), and "with a love"(line 11), shows
    (A) the absence of variety in passionate love
    (B) the lack of fervor in the poet's words
    (C) the restraint the lover feels
    (D) a confident and sure declaration of love and passion
    (E) an overconfident and rather smug love

268. "I love thee freely, as men strive for right" (line 7) shows that she loves him
    (A) with obligation
    (B) with a love that is forced
    (C) with some constraint, guilt, and force
    (D) out of resolute pity
    (E) as humans strive for what is necessary to achieve happiness

269. The words "being"(line 4), "grace"(line 4), "right" (line 7), and "praise" (line 8) are emphasized to show
    (A) personification
    (B) the divine
    (C) the stridently metaphorical
    (D) each as an image
    (E) the ultimate in loving another person

270. In the poetic sentence "I love thee with a passion put to use / In my old griefs, and with my childhood's faith" (lines 9–10), "put to use" means that
    (A) only the love is put to use
    (B) above all, the passion is put to use
    (C) the old grief is put to use
    (D) childhood faith is put to use
    (E) passion, grief, and faith are needed for love

271. "I seemed to lose / With my lost saints" (lines 11–12) suggests
    (A) her disillusionment
    (B) a love she seemed to lose
    (C) her lost love and lost saints
    (D) that she loves in place of her religion
    (E) that she loves as fervently as she practices her religion

272. The love described in the poem goes through stages, moving from
    (A) hope, to loss, to gain
    (B) intensity, to innocence, to frustration
    (C) profit, to loss, to resourcefulness
    (D) range, to escape, to a supine position
    (E) infatuation, to engagement, to marriage

273. The words "and, if God choose, / I shall but love thee better after death" (lines 13–14) imply
    I. specific heretical concerns
    II. spiritual implications
    III. the physical transitory surroundings
    (A) I only
    (B) II only
    (C) III only
    (D) I and III only
    (E) II and III only

274. The volta, or "turn," of the sonnet comes between
    (A) lines 4 and 5
    (B) lines 13 and 14
    (C) lines 8 and 9
    (D) lines 3 and 4
    (E) lines 7 and 8

See page 132 for the answers to this set of questions.

READING 22: EXCERPT FROM *THE SANDBOX* BY EDWARD ALBEE

QUESTIONS 275–289. Carefully read the following passage, from the first scene, before choosing your answers.

MOMMY (*out over the audience*). Be quiet, Grandma . . . just be quiet, and wait. (GRANDMA *throws a shovelful of sand at* MOMMY. *Still out over the audience*) She's throwing sand at me! You stop that, Grandma; you stop throwing sand at Mommy! (*To* DADDY) She's throwing sand at me.   5
(DADDY *looks around at* GRANDMA, *who screams at him.*)

GRANDMA. GRAAAAAA!

MOMMY. Don't look at her. Just . . . sit here . . . be very still . . . and wait. (*To the* MUSICIAN) You . . . uh . . . you go ahead and do whatever it is you do. (*The* MUSICIAN *plays.*   10
MOMMY *and* DADDY *are fixed, staring out beyond the audience.* GRANDMA *looks at them, looks at the* MUSICIAN, *looks at the sandbox, throws down the shovel.*)

GRANDMA. Ah-haaaaaa! Graaaaaa! (*Looks for reaction; gets none. Now . . . directly to the audience*) Honestly! What a   15
way to treat an old woman! Drag her out of the house . . . stick her in a car . . . bring her out here from the city . . . dump her in a pile of sand . . . and leave her here to set. I'm eighty-six years old! I was married when I was seventeen. To a farmer. He died when I was thirty. (*To the*   20
MUSICIAN) Will you stop that, please? (*The* MUSICIAN *stops playing.*) I'm a feeble old woman . . . how do you expect anybody to hear me over that peep! peep! peep! (*To herself*) There's no respect around here (*To the* YOUNG MAN) There's no respect around here!   25

YOUNG MAN (*same smile*). Hi!

GRANDMA (*after a pause, a mild double-take, continues, to the audience*). My husband died when I was thirty (*indicates* MOMMY), and I had to raise that big cow over there all by my lonesome. You can imagine what *that was like.* Lordy!   30
(*To the* YOUNG MAN) Where'd they get *you?*

YOUNG MAN. Oh . . . I've been around for a while.

GRANDMA. I'll bet you have! Heh, heh, heh. Will you look at you!

YOUNG MAN (*flexing his muscles*). Isn't that something?   35
(*Continues his calisthenics.*)

GRANDMA. Boy, oh boy; I'll say. Pretty good.

YOUNG MAN (*sweetly*) I'll say.

GRANDMA. Where ya from?

YOUNG MAN. Southern California.   40

GRANDMA (*nodding*). Figgers; figgers. What's your name, honey?

YOUNG MAN. I don't know . . .

GRANDMA (*to the audience*). Bright, too!

YOUNG MAN. I mean . . . I mean, they haven't given me one   45
yet . . . the studio . . .

275. "What a way to treat an old woman! Drag her out of the house . . . stick her in a car . . . bring her out here from the city . . . dump her in a pile of sand . . . and leave her here to set" (lines 15–18) seems to show
  (A) an absurdist's view of the way old people are treated
  (B) life at the beach
  (C) a realist's view of the way old people are treated
  (D) hope for the future
  (E) a pragmatist's view of the way old people are treated

276. The entire passage shows that the author encourages the audience to
  (A) laugh harshly at children at play
  (B) cry sweetly for a misspent youth
  (C) laugh bitterly and draw attention to a dysfunctional family
  (D) smile blithely at life
  (E) stop going to the beach

277. "Will you stop that, please?" (line 21) is addressed to the Musician. All of the following apply to this line EXCEPT
  (A) the play deals with a beginning-of-life ritual
  (B) the actors talk to the sound people
  (C) the situation is absurd
  (D) Grandma appears to be a senile dementia extrovert
  (E) absurd drama philosophically addresses even staging limitations

278. "GRANDMA (nodding). Figgers; figgers. What's your name, honey?
  YOUNG MAN. I don't know . . .
  GRANDMA (to the audience). Bright, too!" (lines 41–44)
  This repartee shows all of the following EXCEPT
  (A) 86-year-old Grandma still has a sense of humor
  (B) the Young Man is intellectually gifted
  (C) the Young Man appears to lack knowledge
  (D) Grandma's bantering fakes an entree into romance
  (E) Grandma's term "Honey" aids her obviously feigned seduction

279. The interlinear scene direction in line 13, "(looks at the sandbox, throws down the shovel)," indicates a subtext that includes all of the following EXCEPT
  (A) because of their treatment old people often simply give up
  (B) Mommy and Daddy needed to be shocked back to reality
  (C) Mommy and Daddy have reacted to Grandma appropriately
  (D) aggressive tendencies of senility are often fleeting
  (E) drama, even absurd drama, is often allegorical

280. When Mommy says, "She's throwing sand at me! You stop that, Grandma; you stop throwing sand at Mommy! (To DADDY) She's throwing sand at me" (lines 3–5), the indication is that Albee
  (A) shows in Mommy's words and actions a loving daughter
  (B) shows that Mommy hates Daddy
  (C) holds a comic mirror up to family relationships
  (D) shows that Daddy really hates Mommy
  (E) seriously depicts matricide

281. In line 29, the "big cow" is
    (A) Grandma
    (B) Daddy
    (C) the Young Man
    (D) Mommy
    (E) the sandbox

282. The entire excerpt shows
    (A) nastiness and lack of kindness on the part of Mommy and
        Daddy
    (B) no empathy at all for Grandma
    (C) empathy for Mommy and Daddy
    (D) empathy for the Young Man
    (E) real love in this strange family

283. The sandbox itself is
    (A) symbolic of the womb
    (B) representative of the grave
    (C) symbolic of youthful days at the beach
    (D) representative of American soil
    (E) symbolic of our nascent salad days

284. *The Sandbox* addresses all of the following EXCEPT
    (A) the poverty of interpersonal communication
    (B) the essence of theater itself in modern America
    (C) the idea that the limitations of symbolic drama in our media-
        driven society may also be its greatest asset
    (D) the poor treatment of old people once they are deemed to
        have no value to society
    (E) the idea that no truly great and seminal ideas can ever come
        from comedy but must originate in tragedy

285. In a most absurd way, the play deals with
    I. an elderly parent, treated as an infant by her family,
        protesting her fate
    II. the fact that the roles have changed and the child has now
        become the parent who is confronting an awareness of death
    III. the fact that the elderly are mocked as being closer to death
    (A) I only
    (B) I and II only
    (C) II and III only
    (D) I, II, and III
    (E) II only

286. In lines 16–17, "Drag her out of the house . . . stick her in a car,"
    the "her" referred to is
    (A) Mommy
    (B) Grandma
    (C) the sandbox
    (D) the Musician
    (E) an unknown victim

287. The word "figgers" (line 41) is
    (A) a made-up word mimicking the sounds of the words for "it figures"
    (B) slang for "you have a nice figure"
    (C) a colloquialism for "it does not compute"
    (D) dialect for "fantastically bigger"
    (E) lingo for "a beach bum"

288. "[T]hat peep! peep! peep!" (line 23) is an example of
    (A) oxymoron
    (B) an image of baby chickens
    (C) onomatopoeia
    (D) an image of sight
    (E) a friend on the Internet and the phone

289. The words "that was like" are italicized in line 30 because they
    (A) are just another interlinear scene direction
    (B) indicate to the actor to say them silently
    (C) indicate to the actor to sing them
    (D) indicate to the actor to show optimistic merriment
    (E) indicate to the actor to stress sarcasm

See page 133 for the answers to this set of questions.

READING 23: "TO HIS COY MISTRESS" BY ANDREW MARVELL

QUESTIONS 290–299. Carefully read the poem before choosing your answers.

Had we but world enough, and time,
This coyness, lady, were no crime.
We would sit down, and think which way
To walk, and pass our long love's day.
Thou by the Indian Ganges' side   5
Shouldst rubies find; I by the tide
Of Humber would complain. I would
Love you ten years before the Flood,
And you should, if you please, refuse
Till the conversion of the Jews.   10
My vegetable love should grow
Vaster than empires, and more slow;
An hundred years should go to praise
Thine eyes, and on thy forehead gaze;
Two hundred to adore each breast,   15
But thirty thousand to the rest;
An age at least to every part,
And the last age should show your heart.
For, lady, you deserve this state,
Nor would I love at lower rate.   20
    But at my back I always hear
Time's wingèd chariot hurrying near;
And yonder all before us lie
Deserts of vast eternity.
Thy beauty shall no more be found,   25
Nor, in thy marble vault, shall sound
My echoing song; then worms shall try
That long preserved virginity,
And your quaint honor turn to dust,
And into ashes all my lust: 30
The grave's a fine and private place,
But none, I think, do there embrace.
    Now therefore, while the youthful hue
Sits on thy skin like morning dew,
And while thy willing soul transpires   35
At every pore with instant fires,
Now let us sport us while we may,
And now, like amorous birds of prey,
Rather at once our time devour
Than languish in his slow-chapped power.   40
Let us roll all our strength and all
Our sweetness up into one ball,
And tear our pleasures with rough strife
Thorough the iron gates of life.
Thus, though we cannot make our sun   45
Stand still, yet we will make him run.

290. The meter of the poem is
    (A) trochaic
    (B) spondaic
    (C) dactyllic
    (D) iambic tetrameter
    (E) iambic pentameter

291. The predominant rhyme scheme is
    (A) internal
    (B) feminine
    (C) masculine
    (D) free verse
    (E) oblique

292. The three stanzas together comprise a
    (A) concession, speculation, assertion
    (B) supposition, stipulation, settlement
    (C) thesis, antithesis, synthesis
    (D) premise, second premise, conclusion
    (E) proposal, counterproposal, compromise

293. The first stanza includes all of the following EXCEPT
    (A) hyperbole
    (B) simile
    (C) allusion
    (D) imagery
    (E) metaphor

294. A metaphysical idea is compared to a concrete object in all of the following lines EXCEPT
    (A) 11
    (B) 15
    (C) 29
    (D) 30
    (E) 35–36

295. The persona of the narrator could best be described as
    (A) ignominious
    (B) dogmatic
    (C) gloomy
    (D) witty
    (E) compliant

296. The tone of the poem shifts from
    (A) facetious, to admonitory, to beseeching
    (B) mocking, to pedantic, to amorous
    (C) boorish, to despairing, to assuaged
    (D) adulatory, to lustful, to companionable
    (E) heroic, to counseling, to conciliatory

297. The poem expresses the sentiment of which of the following
     aphorisms?
     (A) It is better to have loved and lost than never to have loved at
         all.
     (B) Seize the day.
     (C) Love is blind.
     (D) Be always faithful.
     (E) To thine own self be true.

298. In the line "For, lady, you deserve this state" (line 19), "state"
     most closely means
     (A) civility
     (B) dominion
     (C) pageantry
     (D) obeisance
     (E) predicament

299. "Rather at once our time devour / Than languish in his slow-
     chapped power" (lines 39–40) most closely means that the lovers
     should be
     (A) amatory, not acrimonious
     (B) confederate, not discordant
     (C) refractory, not obsequious
     (D) decorous, not licentious
     (E) audacious, not acquiescent

See page 133 for the answers to this set of questions.

READING 24: "DO NOT GO GENTLE INTO THAT GOOD NIGHT" BY DYLAN THOMAS

QUESTIONS 300–314. Carefully read the poem before choosing your answers.

Do not go gentle into that good night,
Old age should burn and rave at close of day;
Rage, rage against the dying of the light.

Though wise men at their end know dark is right,
Because their words had forked no lightning they   5
Do not go gentle into that good night.

Good men, the last wave by, crying how bright
Their frail deeds might have danced in a green bay,
Rage, rage against the dying of the light.

Wild men who caught and sang the sun in flight,   10
And learn, too late, they grieved it on its way,
Do not go gentle into that good night.

Grave men, near death, who see with blinding sight
Blind eyes could blaze like meteors and be gay,
Rage, rage against the dying of the light.   15

And you, my father, there on the sad height,
Curse, bless, me now with your fierce tears, I pray,
Do not go gentle into that good night.
Rage, rage against the dying of the light.

300. This poem is concerned with
    (A) death and dying
    (B) the relationship between parent and child
    (C) journeys and music
    (D) both (A) and (B)
    (E) both (B) and (C)

301. The entire poem is an example of the
    (A) French villanelle
    (B) English sonnet
    (C) Italian sonnet
    (D) Greek aubade
    (E) French alexandrine

302. "Old age should burn and rave at close of day" (line 2)
    metaphorically suggests
    (A) a physical connection between fire and sunshine
    (B) a philosophical association between start and finish
    (C) an opinion that the old and infirm should remain vigorous
        and assertive and not acquiesce to death
    (D) a theological connection between the future and freshness
    (E) that young people have no understanding of death

303. "Good men, the last wave by, crying how bright / Their frail deeds
     might have danced in a green bay, / Rage, rage against the dying
     of the light" (lines 7–9) suggests
     (A) frail waters and merriment
     (B) deeds reflecting and shining
     (C) waves sobbing and blithe
     (D) despair saturated with lamentation
     (E) that tears reflect whatever is around them

304. "Wild men who caught and sang the sun in flight, / And learn,
     too late, they grieved it on its way" (lines 10–11) refers to the fact
     that
     (A) no escapades can shine and dazzle like the sun
     (B) no actions can be thought of as optimistic
     (C) all grief comes unannounced and late
     (D) many actions are particularly filled with grief
     (E) all sorrow comes when we least expect it

305. "Grave men, near death, who see with blinding sight / Blind eyes
     could blaze like meteors and be gay, / Rage, rage against the
     dying of the light" (lines 13–15) indicates
     (A) happiness
     (B) sadness
     (C) dementia
     (D) Alzheimer's disease
     (E) sparseness

306. In stanza 6, lines 16–19, the poet asks
     (A) that those around not scream at death
     (B) that those around bless his father and cry when death comes
     (C) that his father not curse death
     (D) for a paternal endorsement of wrath and fury
     (E) that his father be happy when death comes

307. In line 13, the word "grave" is a noteworthy example of
     (A) an oxymoron
     (B) a pun
     (C) a sepulcher
     (D) a sedated person
     (E) a cemetery

308. Thomas considers different types of men in each stanza. He uses
     the adjectives "wise" (line 4), "good"(line 7), "wild" (line 10), and
     "grave" (line 13). This progression shows that all dying men
     (A) could not have done more
     (B) should not seize the moment
     (C) should accept fate
     (D) should capture what the moment offers them
     (E) should never set up barriers to the inevitable

309. Lines 1–3 could be restated as
     (A) give up and give in to death easily
     (B) do not protest your passing away
     (C) pray and take your death with ease
     (D) struggle, complain, and rail against your imminent demise
     (E) accept death as something not to fight against

310. The meter of each line of the poem is
    (A) trochaic trimeter
    (B) iambic pentameter
    (C) iambic trimeter
    (D) dactyllic pentameter
    (E) anapestic tetrameter

311. The line "Do not go gentle into that good night" (lines 1, 6, 12, and 18) is repeatedly interspersed with the line "Rage, rage against the dying of the light" (lines 3, 9, 15, 19). The effect on the reader is of the power of
    (A) love over hatred
    (B) God over the Devil
    (C) anger over submission
    (D) resignation over vehemence
    (E) wealth over poverty

312. In line 2, "rave" means
    I. to talk wildly
    II. to utter in a frenzy
    III. to talk or act irrationally, as a madman
    (A) I and III only
    (B) II and III only
    (C) III only
    (D) I, II, and III
    (E) I and II only

313. The pattern of the stanzas is
    (A) five tercets and a quatrain
    (B) six tercets and a couplet
    (C) two quatrains
    (D) interlocking terza rima
    (E) six couplets

314. In the repeated line "Rage, rage against the dying of the light" (lines 3, 9, 15, and 19) the word "rage" cries out for
    (A) absolution
    (B) innocence
    (C) resistance
    (D) naïveté
    (E) confident expectation

See page 133 for the answers to this set of questions.

READING 25: "A SUPERMARKET IN CALIFORNIA" BY ALLEN GINSBERG

QUESTIONS 315–325. Carefully read the poem before choosing your answers.

What thoughts I have of you tonight, Walt
Whitman, for I walked down the sidestreets under the
trees with a headache self-conscious looking at the full
moon.

In my hungry fatigue, and shopping for images, I   5
went into the neon fruit supermarket, dreaming of
your enumerations!

What peaches and what penumbras? Whole
families shopping at night! Aisles full of husbands!
Wives in the avocados, babies in the tomatoes!—and   10
you, García Lorca, what were you doing down by the
watermelons?

I.I I saw you, Walt Whitman, childless, lonely old
grubber, poking among the meats in the refrigerator
and eyeing the grocery boys.   15

I heard you asking questions of each: Who killed
the pork chops? What price bananas? Are you my
Angel?

I wandered in and out of the brilliant stacks of cans
following you, and followed in my imagination by the   20
store detective.

We strode down the open corridors together in
our solitary fancy tasting artichokes, possessing every
frozen delicacy, and never passing the cashier.

Where are we going, Walt Whitman? The doors   25
close in an hour. Which way does your beard point
tonight?

(I touch your book and dream of our odyssey in the
supermarket and feel absurd.)

Will we walk all night through solitary streets? The   30
trees add shade to shade, lights out in the houses, we'll
both be lonely.

Will we stroll dreaming of the lost America of love
past blue automobiles in driveways, home to our silent
cottage?   35

Ah, dear father, graybeard, lonely old courage-
teacher, what America did you have when Charon quit
poling his ferry and you got out on a smoking bank
and stood watching the boat disappear on the black
waters of Lethe?   40

315. The adjective "neon" (line 6) used in the context of a fruit market most significantly connotes
    (A) menace
    (B) sophistication
    (C) vitality
    (D) gaudiness
    (E) bricolage

316. The imagery of the third stanza raises the notion of
    (A) consumerism
    (B) economic colonialism
    (C) religion
    (D) aesthetic influence
    (E) sustenance

317. The poem uses all of the following rhetorical devices EXCEPT
    (A) rhetorical question
    (B) parenthetical aside
    (C) apostrophe
    (D) innuendo
    (E) invective

318. In the second stanza, "tasting artichokes," "possessing every frozen delicacy," and "never passing the cashier" are all
    (A) gerund phrases
    (B) participial phrases
    (C) adjectival clauses
    (D) noun clauses
    (E) prepositional phrases

319. The phrase "dreaming of your enumerations" in the first stanza most closely means
    (A) reflecting on your classification systems
    (B) feeling the loss of your presence
    (C) feeling inspired by your poetic images
    (D) computing a system of numerology
    (E) feeling envious of your metaphors

320. By using the word "odyssey" (line 28), the narrator indicates his feeling that
    (A) life is a challenge
    (B) his journey is coming to an end
    (C) his relationship with Whitman is only imaginary
    (D) he cannot achieve greatness as a poet
    (E) his supermarket experience is of epic proportions

321. The tone of the poem is one of
    (A) lyric nostalgia
    (B) aching loneliness
    (C) bitter reproof
    (D) elevated absurdity
    (E) spent enthusiasm

322. In the final stanza, the poem shifts from
     (A) criticism to homage
     (B) exultant living to death
     (C) melancholy to hope
     (D) sterility to vision
     (E) fantasy to nostalgia

323. The setting of a supermarket
     (A) expresses a distaste for materialism
     (B) bemoans the difficulty of making artistic choices
     (C) equates the artistic world with a marketplace
     (D) honors the entrepreneurial spirit
     (E) mourns the erosion of American democracy

324. In the final stanza, "Charon" (line 37) refers to
     (A) a character from Greek mythology
     (B) a contemporary ferryman
     (C) Walt Whitman
     (D) the poet himself
     (E) another Beat poet

325. The reader can detect Ginsberg's dominant feeling toward
     Whitman in the phrase
     (A) "lonely old grubber" (lines 13–14)
     (B) "eyeing the grocery boys" (line 15)
     (C) "Are you my Angel?" (lines 17–18)
     (D) "lonely old courage-teacher" (lines 36–37)
     (E) "watching the boat disappear on the black waters of Lethe"
         (lines 39–40)

See page 133 for the answers to this set of questions.

READING 26: "THAT TIME OF YEAR THOU MAYST IN ME BEHOLD" BY WILLIAM SHAKESPEARE

QUESTIONS 326–339. Carefully read the poem before choosing your answers.

> That time of year thou mayst in me behold
> When yellow leaves, or none, or few, do hang
> Upon those boughs which shake against the cold,
> Bare ruined choirs, where late the sweet birds sang.
> In me thou see'st the twilight of such day   5
> As after sunset fadeth in the west,
> Which by and by black night doth take away,
> Death's second self that seals up all in rest.
> In me thou see'st the glowing of such fire,
> That on the ashes of his youth doth lie,   10
> As the deathbed whereon it must expire,
> Consumed with that which it was nourished by.
>   This thou perceiv'st, which makes thy love more strong,
>   To love that well which thou must leave ere long.

326. The poem taken in its totality is a fine example of
  (A) an Italian sonnet
  (B) a Petrarchan sonnet
  (C) a villanelle
  (D) an English sonnet
  (E) an aubade

327. The pivotal images of each quatrain center around
  (A) year, month, week
  (B) season, day, instant
  (C) faith, hope, charity
  (D) death, life, resurrection
  (E) agape, philios, eros

328. The images in the first quatrain (lines 1–4)
  (A) deal exclusively with falling leaves
  (B) deal solely with empty choir stalls
  (C) deal only with branches devoid of covey and foliage
  (D) offer only figurative examples of leaves, stalls, branches
  (E) offer no reminders of figurative language

329. The major grammatical and structural divisions occur in the following patterns
  (A) lines 1–4; 5–8; 9–12; 13–14
  (B) lines 1–8; 9–14
  (C) lines 1–12; 13–14
  (D) lines 1–3; 4–6; 7–9; 10–12; 13–14
  (E) lines 1–6; 7–12; 13–14

330. The selection's first grammatically complete sentence is in lines
     1–4, and it has as a main predicate verb
     (A) "Upon" (line 3)
     (B) "do" (line 2)
     (C) "mayst . . . behold" (line 1)
     (D) "shake" (line 3)
     (E) "hang" (line 2)

331. The poem's second grammatically complete sentence, in lines 5–
     8, has as a main predicate verb
     (A) "fadeth" (line 6)
     (B) "see'st" (line 5)
     (C) "doth take" (line 7)
     (D) "seals" (line 8)
     (E) "night" (line 7)

332. The third grammatically complete sentence, lines 9–12, has as a
     main predicate verb
     (A) "glowing" (line 9)
     (B) "lie" (line 10)
     (C) "see'st" (line 9)
     (D) "expire" (line 11)
     (E) "Consumed" (line 12)

333. The main predicate verb in the fourth grammatically complete
     sentence, lines 13–14, is
     (A) "must" (line 14)
     (B) "perceiv'st" (line 13)
     (C) "makes"(line 13)
     (D) "love" (line 14)
     (E) "leave" (line 14)

334. The commonality of the first three major images, one each in the
     three quatrains (lines 1–4, 5–8, and 9–12), is best described as
     (A) ever-decreasing intervals of time
     (B) uplifting and fortunate periods of nature
     (C) edifying and inviolable periods of hope
     (D) gloom and doom epochs of memoirs
     (E) blissful and jocund eras of neglect

335. "When yellow leaves, or none, or few, do hang" (line 2) shows
     (A) religion as the only hope for mankind
     (B) science—especially botany—as the only hope for mankind
     (C) a steady and all-pervasive decline in nature
     (D) an accelerated regeneration of all of nature
     (E) no hope for love or friendship

336. "Consumed with that which it was nourished by" (line 12) refers
     to the
     (A) paradox that the more we die the more we live
     (B) equivocation that hope builds from despair
     (C) thermodynamics of internal combustion
     (D) exuberance of a life-sustaining cosmos
     (E) paradoxical partnership between life and death that is found
         in a symbiotic relationship

337. The theme in the last two lines is best described as
   I. the realization by the lovers that they must eventually die and that death makes their love stronger
   II. the recognition that there is great hope for the future
   III. the awareness that life must be lived only for the moment
   (A) I only
   (B) II and III only
   (C) I and III only
   (D) II only
   (E) III only

338. "Death's second self" (line 8) refers to
   (A) a corpse
   (B) sleep
   (C) rapture
   (D) liability
   (E) embalming

339. "To love that well which thou must leave ere long" (line 14) resolves a contention that is centered around
   (A) the hope youth gives an aging speaker
   (B) the lost youth of an aging speaker
   (C) the despair youth gives an aging speaker
   (D) the maturing hollowness of love
   (E) the continuance of youthful vigor

See page 133 for the answers to this set of questions.

READING 27: "GOD'S GRANDEUR" BY GERARD MANLEY HOPKINS

QUESTIONS 340–354. Carefully read the poem before choosing your answers.

> The world is charged with the grandeur of God.
>   It will flame out, like shining from shook foil;
>   It gathers to a greatness, like the ooze of oil
> Crushed. Why do men then now not reck his rod?
> Generations have trod, have trod, have trod;   5
>   And all is seared with trade; bleared, smeared with toil;
>   And wears man's smudge and shares man's smell: the soil
> Is bare now, nor can foot feel, being shod.
>
> And for all this, nature is never spent;
>   There lives the dearest freshness deep down things;   10
> And though the last lights off the black West went
>   Oh, morning, at the brown brink eastward, springs—
> Because the Holy Ghost over the bent
>   World broods with warm breast and with ah! bright wings.

340. The poem is a(n)
    (A) Spenserian sonnet
    (B) villanelle
    (C) Italian sonnet
    (D) English sonnet
    (E) sestina

341. Line 6 contains
    (A) internal rhyme
    (B) rhyme royal
    (C) anaphora
    (D) anapest
    (E) eye rhyme

342. The poem employs all of the following poetic sound devices, where indicated, EXCEPT
    (A) alliteration in line 2
    (B) enjambment in line 3
    (C) assonance in line 6
    (D) caesura in line 6
    (E) consonance in line 7

343. The primary rhyme form is
    (A) broken rhyme
    (B) masculine rhyme
    (C) feminine rhyme
    (D) eye rhyme
    (E) slant rhyme

344. Lines 1–3 create a sense of
  (A) religious doubt
  (B) the wealth of nations
  (C) the glory of creation
  (D) God's omniscience
  (E) God's devotion to humankind

345. The poem moves from
  (A) problem, to cause of the problem, to solution
  (B) description, to assertion, to exhortation
  (C) earth, to hell, to heaven
  (D) idyll, to lampoon, to requiem
  (E) lyric, to lament, to rhapsody

346. Lines 5–8 represent
  (A) the repetitive cycle of getting and spending
  (B) spiritual alienation resulting from materialism
  (C) Marxist ideas of labor as capital
  (D) repeated plowing of the same field
  (E) gloomy factory work that shrinks souls

347. The line "And for all this, nature is never spent" (line 9) most closely means that nature
  (A) doesn't cost much to enjoy
  (B) doesn't enter into economic transactions
  (C) has been reduced to poverty
  (D) never stops producing its wonders
  (E) is worth the cost of protecting it

348. The poem is most like a(n)
  (A) idyll
  (B) doggerel
  (C) dirge
  (D) psalm
  (E) pastoral

349. The tone of the poem is
  (A) respectful
  (B) rapturous
  (C) reverential
  (D) solemn
  (E) refined

350. The last two lines of the poem evoke connotations of
  (A) birds and angels
  (B) motherhood and pageantry
  (C) holiness and the profane
  (D) guardianship and freedom
  (E) nourishment and vitality

351. The vocabulary of the poem is primarily
  (A) colloquial
  (B) elevated
  (C) Biblical
  (D) ordinary
  (E) esoteric

352. The effect of the phrase "reck his rod" (line 4) relies on the reader's
    (A) familiarity with the Bible
    (B) awareness of the adage "Spare the rod and spoil the child"
    (C) intuitive ability to translate a neologism
    (D) recognition of alliteration
    (E) awareness of British colloquialisms

353. The antecedent to "And wears man's smudge and shares man's smell" (line 7) is
    (A) "The world" (line 1)
    (B) "grandeur of God" (line 1)
    (C) "It" (line 2)
    (D) "Generations" (line 5)
    (E) "all" (line 6)

354. Lines 11–12 refer to the
    (A) harbinger of spring
    (B) rotation of the Earth
    (C) conservation of energy
    (D) dawn of humankind
    (E) fall of the Western world

See page 133 for the answers to this set of questions.

READING 28: "MID-TERM BREAK" BY SEAMUS HEANEY

QUESTIONS 355–367. Carefully read the poem before choosing your answers.

I sat all morning in the college sick bay
Counting bells knelling classes to a close.
At two o'clock our neighbors drove me home.

In the porch I met my father crying—
He had always taken funerals in his stride—   5
And Big Jim Evans saying it was a hard blow.

The baby cooed and laughed and rocked the pram
When I came in, and I was embarrassed
By old men standing up to shake my hand

And tell me they were "sorry for my trouble."   10
Whispers informed strangers I was the eldest,
Away at school, as my mother held my hand

In hers and coughed out angry tearless sighs.
At ten o'clock the ambulance arrived
With the corpse, stanched and bandaged by the nurses.   15

Next morning I went up into the room. Snowdrops
And candles soothed the bedside; I saw him
For the first time in six weeks. Paler now,

Wearing a poppy bruise on his left temple,
He lay in the four foot box as in his cot.   20
No gaudy scars, the bumper knocked him clear.

A four foot box, a foot for every year.

355. The title of this poem is
  (A) definitely epic
  (B) somewhat ironic
  (C) extremely realistic
  (D) recklessly naturalistic
  (E) clandestinely romantic

356. The subject of this poem is the memory of
  (A) a numbing bereavement
  (B) an ostentatious mourning
  (C) an agreeable event
  (D) an unambiguous reminiscence
  (E) a happy time, much to Heaney's chagrin

357. In the phrase "Counting bells knelling classes to a close" (line 2),
the word "knelling" conjures up a sound that is all of the
following EXCEPT
(A) vividly and stridently staccato
(B) slowly and solemnly tolling
(C) strangely upbeat and fanciful
(D) a deliberate and somber tempo
(E) accompanied by sounds of keening

358. The entire poem is an example of
(A) terza rima
(B) enjambment
(C) sonnet
(D) deus ex machina
(E) simple tercet schematics

359. Lines 12 and 13, "as my mother held my hand / In hers and
coughed out angry tearless sighs," are an example of
(A) terza rima
(B) sonnet
(C) enjambment
(D) simile
(E) onomatopoeia

360. Saying "By old men standing up to shake my hand / And tell me
they were 'sorry for my trouble'" (lines 9–10) draws attention to
the
(A) awkwardness and evasion at such events
(B) cacophony at such events
(C) stealth at such events
(D) rapture at such events
(E) church's views of events such as this

361. The word "pram" (line 7) refers to
(A) the baby
(B) the ambulance
(C) the baby's crib
(D) a baby carriage
(E) the hospital bed

362. The poet's emphases on specific words as he moves from "the
corpse, stanched and bandaged," (line 15) to "I saw him (line 17)
... his left temple (line 19) . . . he lay (line 20) . . . his cot. / No
gaudy scars," (lines 20–21) suggests a change from
(A) noninvolvement to involvement
(B) a universal reserve to a specific commitment
(C) nonparticipation to active participation
(D) detached and aloof sharing to active caring
(E) a scientific view to a religious view

363. The poem has a clearly defined formal structure that is composed
of
(A) unrhymed couplets
(B) three-line stanzas with loose iambic meter
(C) three-line stanzas with no meter
(D) three-line stanzas with strict dactylic hexameter
(E) three-line stanzas with strict anapestic trimeter

364. The lines "I saw him / For the first time in six weeks. Paler now, / Wearing a poppy bruise on his left temple" (17–19) show a memory of the death of
    (A) the speaker's father
    (B) the speaker's mother
    (C) the speaker's brother
    (D) Big Jim Evans
    (E) the baby

365. "He lay in the four foot box as in his cot" (line 20) is an example of
    (A) scansion
    (B) hamartia
    (C) simile
    (D) metaphor
    (E) hubris

366. It can be inferred from the description in line 7, "The baby cooed and laughed and rocked the pram," that the sounds are
    (A) not valued by the speaker because they are out of place
    (B) not valued by the speaker because they are not out of place
    (C) valued as a picture of the end of life with no affirmation
    (D) valued as the antithesis to life with affirmation
    (E) valued because they show a sharp contrast, an affirmation of life

367. The final line, "A four foot box, a foot for every year" (line 22), emphasizes
    (A) candidly the great feeling of sadness at last transmitted to the reader
    (B) the grief that the author still hides from the reader
    (C) a faded unimportant memory
    (D) an adult embellishment of a recollection of sadness
    (E) an arithmetic equation

See page 133 for the answers to this set of questions.

READING 29: "BATTER MY HEART, THREE-PERSONED GOD" BY JOHN DONNE

QUESTIONS 368–382. Carefully read the poem before choosing your answers.

> Batter my heart, three-personed God, for You
> As yet but knock, breathe, shine, and seek to mend.
> That I may rise and stand, o'erthrow me, and bend
> Your force to break, blow, burn, and make me new.
> I, like an usurped town to another due,   5
> Labor to admit You, but Oh! to no end.
> Reason, Your viceroy in me, me should defend,
> But is captived, and proves weak or untrue.
> Yet dearly I love You, and would be lovèd fain,
> But am betrothed unto Your enemy;   10
> Divorce me, untie or break that knot again;
> Take me to You, imprison me, for I,
> Except You enthrall me, never shall be free,
> Nor ever chaste, except You ravish me.

368. The "three-personed God" (line 1) is the
(A) poet's interlocutor
(B) Holy Trinity
(C) poet's betrothed
(D) congregation
(E) familial unit

369. Another way to say "would be lovèd fain" (line 9) is
(A) would be loved faithfully
(B) will love you for all time
(C) love will not be requited
(D) would happily be loved
(E) will be loved weakly

370. Who is the usurper?
(A) the narrator
(B) the town
(C) the betrothed
(D) Satan
(E) God

371. Lines 9–14 form a(n)
(A) spondee
(B) dactyl
(C) sestet
(D) trochee
(E) anapest

372. The paradox in the first quatrain is the idea of
    (A) destroying to be reborn
    (B) subduing to overthrow
    (C) rising to mend
    (D) battering to bend
    (E) blowing to burn

373. The first four lines are notable for their
    (A) lyricism
    (B) proliferation of verbs
    (C) irreverent tone
    (D) religious piety
    (E) second-person addressee

374. The meter of the poem is primarily
    (A) iambic tetrameter
    (B) trochaic
    (C) anapestic
    (D) alexandrine
    (E) iambic pentameter

375. All the following lines are paradoxical EXCEPT
    (A) "That I may rise and stand, o'erthrow me" (line 3)
    (B) "Your force to break . . . make me new" (line 4)
    (C) "Labor to admit You, but Oh! to no end" (line 6)
    (D) "Except You enthrall me, never shall be free" (line 13)
    (E) "Nor ever chaste, except You ravish me" (line 14)

376. The poem includes all of the following EXCEPT
    (A) metaphor
    (B) pun
    (C) personification
    (D) alliteration
    (E) simile

377. The primary metaphysical conceits included in the poem concern
    (A) war, trial, and imprisonment
    (B) war and marriage
    (C) labor and reason
    (D) viceroy and usurper
    (E) chastity and betrothal

378. The verb tense mood in the first line is
    (A) conditional
    (B) affirmative
    (C) negative
    (D) imperative
    (E) subjunctive

379. The "enemy" of line 10 is
    (A) God
    (B) the narrator
    (C) those who surround the town
    (D) the betrothed
    (E) Satan

380. The poem takes the form of a(n)
    (A) rondeau
    (B) idyll
    (C) mock epic
    (D) sonnet
    (E) hymn

381. The tone of the poem is
    (A) imperious
    (B) admonishing
    (C) laudatory
    (D) imploring
    (E) resolute

382. The main idea of the poem can best be expressed as
    (A) Force me to revere you, God
    (B) My devotion is a form of imprisonment
    (C) God's power captivates me
    (D) Devotion supplants reason
    (E) My faith in God has weakened

See page 134 for the answers to this set of questions.

READING 30: "AMERICA" BY CLAUDE MCKAY

QUESTIONS: 383–393. Carefully read the poem before choosing your answers.

> Although she feeds me bread of bitterness,
> And sinks into my throat her tiger's tooth,
> Stealing my breath of life, I will confess
> I love this cultured hell that tests my youth!
> Her vigor flows like tides into my blood,   5
> Giving me strength erect against her hate.
> Her bigness sweeps my being like a flood.
> Yet as a rebel fronts a king in state,
> I stand within her walls with not a shred
> Of terror, malice, not a word of jeer.   10
> Darkly I gaze into the days ahead,
> And see her might and granite wonders there,
> Beneath the touch of Time's unerring hand,
> Like priceless treasures sinking in the sand.

383. The poem is an example of a(n)
    (A) epistle
    (B) villanelle
    (C) terza rima
    (D) sestina
    (E) sonnet

384. The phrase "cultured hell" (line 4) is an example of a(n)
    (A) oxymoron
    (B) aphorism
    (C) portmanteau
    (D) hyperbole
    (E) double entendre

385. The poem appeals mostly to the senses of
    (A) hearing and sight
    (B) taste and touch
    (C) sight and touch
    (D) smell and sight
    (E) smell and touch

386. The poetic meter is primarily
    (A) medial trochee
    (B) spondee rhythm
    (C) sprung rhythm
    (D) iambic pentameter
    (E) dactyl

387. The beginning of the poem through "... breath of life" (lines 1–3)
is a(n)
(A) noun clause
(B) adverb clause
(C) participial phrase
(D) compound sentence
(E) adjective clause

388. The rhyme scheme is primarily
(A) terza rima
(B) feminine rhyme
(C) masculine rhyme
(D) internal rhyme
(E) Sapphic rhyme

389. The narrator asserts that the aspect of America that strengthens
him is its
(A) " cultured hell" (line 4)
(B) "vigor" (line 5)
(C) "hate" (line 6)
(D) "bigness" (line 7)
(E) "might" (line 12)

390. The tone of the poem is primarily one of
(A) repressed rage
(B) bold rebellion
(C) elevated pedantry
(D) frank confession
(E) apologetic contempt

391. The last four lines of the poem include all of the following
EXCEPT
(A) heroic couplet
(B) personification
(C) alliteration
(D) trochee
(E) simile

392. The poem moves from
(A) confession to prophecy
(B) concession to synthesis
(C) thesis to antithesis
(D) exhortation to proclamation
(E) inquisition to decree

393. The central idea of the poem is best expressed by which of the
following statements made by James Baldwin?
(A) If we are not capable of [self-]examination, we may yet
become one of the most distinguished and monumental
failures in the history of nations.
(B) I love America more than any other country in this world,
and, exactly for this reason, I insist on the right to criticize
her perpetually.
(C) I am what time, circumstance, history, have made of me,
certainly, but I am also, much more than that.
(D) The most dangerous creation of any society is the man who
has nothing to lose.
(E) Any writer . . . feels that the world into which he was born is
nothing less than a conspiracy against the cultivation of his
talent.

See page 134 for the answers to this set of questions.

READING 31: "THE CLOD AND THE PEBBLE" BY WILLIAM BLAKE

QUESTIONS 394–407. Carefully read the poem before choosing your answers.

"Love seeketh not Itself to please,
Nor for itself hath any care;
But for another gives its ease,
And builds a Heaven in Hell's despair."

So sang a little Clod of Clay,   5
Trodden with the cattle's feet:
But a Pebble of the brook,
Warbled out these meters meet.

"Love seeketh only Self to please,
To bind another to its delight,   10
Joys in another's loss of ease,
And builds a Hell in Heaven's despite."

394. The entire poem is a(n)
   (A) monograph on disparate categories of amorous commitment
   (B) treatise on contrasted approaches to life and infatuation
   (C) affirmation of various kinds of hostilities
   (D) invective on distinct levels of antipathy
   (E) study of only the amoral and corrupt aspects of love

395. Based on the rhyme scheme, Blake's poem is a fine example of a(n)
   (A) metrical romance
   (B) old ballad
   (C) Italian lyric
   (D) French ballade
   (E) Elizabethan sonnet

396. The clod (line 5) versus the pebble (line 7) is symbolic of
   (A) heartiness versus infirmity
   (B) failure versus success
   (C) altruism versus selfishness
   (D) infatuation versus dislike
   (E) property versus poverty

397. The poem deals with ideas that show
   (A) the self-sacrificing clod contrasted with the selfish pebble
   (B) two views that can be patterned into something different for everyone
   (C) two views of people: those with an idealistic view of the world and those without such a view
   (D) (A), (B), and (C)
   (E) (A) and (B) only

398. The word "Clod" (line 5) is used to imply which of the following?
    (A) a lump of malleable earth
    (B) something unconditionally entrenched with altruism
    (C) an unselfish impression benefiting an often cruel world
    (D) giving up everything for love
    (E) giving up nothing for love

399. The word "Pebble" (line 7) as used in the poem figuratively implies
    (A) a pellet burnished by a motion that wears it down
    (B) a person who experienced aggression
    (C) that an appropriate love must be inaccessible
    (D) resisting all infatuation
    (E) not resisting love, even self-love

400. The poet uses two quotations (lines 1–4 and lines 9–12), each with its own stanza. This is an example of
    (A) the use of religious agape, the worldly eros, and the fraternal philos
    (B) the use of personification—two inanimate objects are speaking
    (C) the use of the real essence of rhetorical questioning
    (D) the use of metonymy
    (E) the use of synecdoche

401. The three major participants in this poem are
    (A) God, man, Satan
    (B) clod, pebble, love
    (C) hatred, wealth, compliance
    (D) death, life, purgatory
    (E) heaven, hell, limbo

402. The word "Trodden" (line 6) suggests that the
    (A) pebble has been crushed
    (B) clod remains firm
    (C) clod has been beaten and shattered
    (D) pebble has been beaten and shattered
    (E) pebble is used to build a road

403. Line 12, "And builds a Hell in Heaven's despite,'" makes clear the author's view that
    (A) we humans can often make our own Heaven by the way we think
    (B) we humans can often make our own Hell by the way we think
    (C) cattle feet and brooks are heavenly images
    (D) despair is an impermanent quality
    (E) both Hell and Heaven are transient

404. The poem taken in its entirety suggests that if you love selflessly, you can
    I. overcome the hardest obstacles
    II. "build a Heaven in Hell's despair"
    III. enjoy a message of hope against reality
    (A) I and III only
    (B) II and III only
    (C) I and II only
    (D) I, II, and III
    (E) III only

405. The poem suggests a contention between two visions. With respect to each vision, all of the following are accurate EXCEPT
    (A) they are blatantly filled with accuracy
    (B) they are conspicuously untrue
    (C) they are philosophically correct
    (D) they are argumentatively and logically legitimate
    (E) they are definitely not specious

406. Sounds and locations aid the images of the poem and are illustrated and suggested by which of the following polarities?
    (A) loam versus brook
    (B) Heaven versus Hell
    (C) song versus harshness
    (D) hardness versus softness
    (E) possessions versus need

407. The Clod (line 5) and the Pebble (line 7) show that
    (A) they each have the power to transform mankind; we are capable of choosing either one
    (B) they each have the power to modify the cosmos; we are predestined
    (C) they can't have any real power over our lives
    (D) love that does not hurt is true
    (E) God is present in rocks and pebbles

See page 134 for the answers to this set of questions.

READING 32: "MEN AT FORTY" BY DONALD JUSTICE

QUESTIONS 408–418. Carefully read the poem before choosing your answers.

Men at forty
Learn to close softly
The doors to rooms they will not be
Coming back to.

At rest on a stair landing,   5
They feel it
Moving beneath them now like the deck of a ship,
Though the swell is gentle.

And deep in mirrors
They rediscover   10
The face of the boy as he practices tying
His father's tie there in secret

And the face of that father,
Still warm with the mystery of lather.
They are more fathers than sons themselves now.   15
Something is filling them, something

That is like the twilight sound
Of the crickets, immense,
Filling the woods at the foot of the slope
Behind their mortgaged houses.   20

408. The first stanza includes all of the following EXCEPT
(A) an adjective clause
(B) enjambment
(C) a metaphor
(D) an infinitive phrase
(E) hyperbole

409. Line 3 is longer than the rest of the lines in the first stanza to
embody in language the sense of a(n)
(A) reluctance to move on
(B) declining physical strength
(C) urge to deflect unwanted ideas
(D) need to remain aloof
(E) desire to move forward in life

410. Men at forty close doors "softly" (line 2) because of their
(A) desire for privacy
(B) reverence for fading memories
(C) resistance to accepting fate
(D) compunction not to disturb others
(E) fastidiousness about housekeeping

411. In the phrase "They feel it" (line 6), "it" most closely means their
    (A) ebbing strength
    (B) unbidden fear
    (C) swelling pride
    (D) declining mental acuity
    (E) remorse over the past

412. The theme of the poem is
    (A) mourning a lost parent
    (B) regret for a life not fully lived
    (C) the power of familial bonds
    (D) acceptance of the aging process
    (E) the dual nature of manhood

413. The tone of the poem is
    (A) dejected
    (B) pensive
    (C) urgent
    (D) pragmatic
    (E) remorseful

414. The poem moves from
    (A) the superficial to the profound
    (B) past to present
    (C) early to later stages of grief
    (D) disquiet to composure
    (E) mortal to spiritual considerations

415. The poet chose the age of forty because it represents a conventional time of
    (A) steep physical decline
    (B) retirement
    (C) peak performance
    (D) wisdom
    (E) transition

416. The word "mortgaged" (line 20) connotes
    (A) a price not yet fully paid
    (B) being in debt to nature
    (C) a life lived responsibly
    (D) following the conventional life path
    (E) being committed to success

417. The poem uses all of the following poetic devices EXCEPT
    (A) simile
    (B) cacophony
    (C) enjambment
    (D) alliteration
    (E) metaphor

418. The ideas of this poem are most closely expressed by which of the following quotations?
    (A) "Those who love deeply never grow old; they may die of old age, but they die young." —Benjamin Franklin
    (B) "From the middle of life onward, only he remains vitally alive who is ready to die with life." —Carl Jung
    (C) "Old age is the most unexpected of all the things that can happen to a man." —Leon Trotsky
    (D) "Don't just count your years; make your years count." —Ernest Meyers
    (E) "The more sand has escaped from the hourglass of our life, the clearer we should see through it." —Jean-Paul Sartre

See page 134 for the answers to this set of questions.

READING 33: EXCERPT FROM "BARTLEBY THE SCRIVENER: A STORY OF WALL STREET" BY HERMAN MELVILLE

Questions 419–432. Carefully read the passage, from the beginning of the short story, before choosing your answers.

I am a rather elderly man. The nature of my avocations for the last thirty years has brought me into more than ordinary contact with what would seem an interesting and somewhat singular set of men of whom as yet nothing that I know of has ever been written—I mean the law-copyists or scriveners. I [5] have known very many of them, professionally and privately, and if I pleased could relate diverse histories at which good-natured gentlemen might smile and sentimental souls might weep. But I waive the biographies of all other scriveners for a few passages in the life of Bartleby, who was a scrivener of [10] the strangest I ever saw or heard of. While of other law-copyists I might write the complete life, of Bartleby nothing of that sort can be done. I believe that no materials exist for a full and satisfactory biography of this man. It is an irreparable loss to literature. Bartleby was one of those beings of whom [15] nothing is ascertainable except from the original sources, and in his case those are very small. What my own astonished eyes saw of Bartleby, *that* is all I know of him except, indeed, one vague report which will appear in the sequel.

Ere introducing the scrivener as he first appeared to me, [20] it is fit I make some mention of myself, my employees, my business, my chambers, and general surroundings, because some such description is indispensable to an adequate understanding of the chief character about to be presented.

Imprimis: I am a man who from his youth upwards has [25] been filled with a profound conviction that the easiest way of life is the best. Hence, though I belong to a profession proverbially energetic and nervous, even to turbulence at times, yet nothing of that sort have I ever suffered to invade my peace. I am one of those unambitious lawyers who never [30] addresses a jury or in any way draws down public applause, but in the cool tranquility of a snug retreat do a snug business among rich men's bonds and mortgages and title-deeds. All who know me consider me an eminently *safe* man. The late John Jacob Astor, a personage little given to poetic [35] enthusiasm, had no hesitation in pronouncing my first grand point to be prudence; my next, method. I do not speak it in vanity but simply record the fact that I was not unemployed in my profession by the late John Jacob Astor, a name which, I admit, I love to repeat, for it hath a rounded and orbicular [40] sound to it and rings like unto bullion. I will freely add that I was not insensible to the late John Jacob Astor's good opinion.

Sometime prior to the period at which this little history begins, my 40 avocations had been largely increased. The good old office now extinct in the State of New York of a Master in Chancery had been conferred upon me. It was not a very arduous office but very pleasantly remunerative. I seldom lose my temper; much more seldom indulge in dangerous indignation at wrongs and outrages; but I must be permitted to 41 be rash here and declare that I consider the sudden and violent abrogation of the office of Master in Chancery by the new Constitution as a _____ premature act, inasmuch as I had counted upon a life-lease of the profits, whereas I only received those of a few short years. But this is by the way. 45

50

55

419. From the context clues in this excerpt the reader knows that a person who is a scrivener does all of the following duties EXCEPT
(A) copy manuscripts
(B) act as a writer
(C) is paid for exact transcription
(D) is noted for penmanship
(E) guard against a bully

420. The storyteller is
(A) an observer who is not omnipotent
(B) a lawyer
(C) a man named Bartleby
(D) a man named Melville
(E) an observer who is not an omnivore

421. In line 25, the word "Imprimis" means
(A) in conclusion
(B) in the first place
(C) in moderation
(D) inconsequential
(E) insipid and lethargic

422. "But I waive the biographies of all other scriveners for a few passages in the life of Bartleby" (lines 9–10) indicates that
   I. Bartleby is unique
   II. Bartleby is strange
   III. the boss admires Bartleby
(A) I only
(B) II only
(C) I and II only
(D) III only
(E) II and III only

423. "I believe that no materials exist for a full and satisfactory biography of this man. It is an irreparable loss to literature" (lines 13–15) expresses the storyteller's
(A) fear of Bartleby
(B) admiration for Bartleby
(C) hidden discontent with the Bartleby situation
(D) veiled threat against Bartleby's life
(E) love of corporate greed

424. "[A] profound conviction that the easiest way of life is the best" (lines 26–27) refers to the
    (A) occupation of scrivener in the way he works
    (B) legal profession in the manner the narrator works it
    (C) profession of journalists in the way it works
    (D) profession of John Jacob Astor and how he worked
    (E) profession of politics and the way it works

425. In line 44, the phrase "this little history" refers to the
    (A) historical account of the life of John Jacob Astor
    (B) historical account of the firm
    (C) historical account of all scriveners
    (D) story concerning Bartleby
    (E) life of Herman Melville

426. In lines 54, the "rash" behavior is directed at
    (A) the fact that Bartleby works there
    (B) the sudden and violent abolition of the office of Master in Chancery
    (C) the happy ending of the office of Master in Chancery
    (D) the fact that the scriveners are all overworked and underpaid
    (E) the fact that members of the legal profession are lazy

427. In the context of lines 30–33, the word "snug" refers to
    (A) the conformable aspects of the situation thus far
    (B) the black comedy of the piece
    (C) the lack of clarity in the situation
    (D) the tight fit between the storyteller and Bartleby
    (E) working hard for the money

428. The phrase "in pronouncing my first grand point to be prudence; my next, method" (lines 36–37) shows
    (A) the narrator's interpretation of John Jacob Astor's view of the narrator
    (B) that Bartleby was a great worker
    (C) that Melville is being humorous
    (D) that God does not seem to be on Bartleby's side
    (E) that God does not seem to be on the storyteller's side

429. "I will freely add that I was not insensible to the late John Jacob Astor's good opinion" (lines 41–43) stresses to the reader that the teller of the tale
    (A) is proud of all his scriveners
    (B) is being self-congratulatory due to the expressed opinion of a well-respected colleague
    (C) is proud of himself
    (D) is proud of Bartleby's work ethic
    (E) hates John Jacob Astor

430. An underlying theme for this selection is
    (A) legality trumps hard work
    (B) a revelation of class prejudice
    (C) cleanliness is next to godliness
    (D) hard work trumps legality
    (E) religion improves society

431. The narrator's mention of "a name which, I admit, I love to repeat, for it hath a rounded and orbicular sound to it" (lines 39–41) does all of the following EXCEPT
    (A) carry the weight of prominence and importance
    (B) evoke the idea of money
    (C) carry a hidden significance
    (D) indicate name dropping
    (E) testify to diminution

432. In the context of lines 44–45, the word "avocation" connotes
    (A) a full-time job or work
    (B) a profession
    (C) a part-time distraction or diversion
    (D) the task of a scribe
    (E) the position of one who cleans the office

See page 134 for the answers to this set of questions.

READING 34: "MY LAST DUCHESS"
BY ROBERT BROWNING

QUESTIONS 433–447. Carefully read the poem before choosing your answers.

Ferrara

That's my last Duchess painted on the wall,
Looking as if she were alive. I call
That piece a wonder, now: Frà Pandolf's hands
Worked busily a day, and there she stands.
Will't please you sit and look at her? I said   5
"Frà Pandolf" by design, for never read
Strangers like you that pictured countenance,
The depth and passion of its earnest glance,
But to myself they turned (since none puts by
The curtain I have drawn for you, but I)   10
And seemed as they would ask me, if they durst,
How such a glance came there; so, not the first
Are you to turn and ask thus. Sir, 'twas not
Her husband's presence only, called that spot
Of joy into the Duchess' cheek: perhaps   15
Frà Pandolf chanced to say "Her mantle laps
Over my lady's wrist too much," or "Paint
Must never hope to reproduce the faint
Half-flush that dies along her throat": such stuff
Was courtesy, she thought, and cause enough   20
For calling up that spot of joy. She had
A heart—how shall I say?—too soon made glad,
Too easily impressed; she liked whate'er
She looked on, and her looks went everywhere.
Sir, 'twas all one! My favor at her breast,   25
The dropping of the daylight in the West,
The bough of cherries some officious fool
Broke in the orchard for her, the white mule
She rode with round the terrace—all and each
Would draw from her alike the approving speech,   30
Or blush, at least. She thanked men,—good! but thanked
Somehow—I know not how—as if she ranked
My gift of a nine-hundred-years-old name
With anybody's gift. Who'd stoop to blame
This sort of trifling? Even had you skill   35
In speech— (which I have not) —to make your will
Quite clear to such an one, and say, "Just this
Or that in you disgusts me; here you miss,
Or there exceed the mark"—and if she let
Herself be lessoned so, nor plainly set   40
Her wits to yours, forsooth, and made excuse,
—E'en then would be some stooping; and I choose
Never to stoop. Oh sir, she smiled, no doubt,
Whene'er I passed her; but who passed without
Much the same smile? This grew; I gave commands;   45

Then all smiles stopped together. There she stands
As if alive. Will't please you rise? We'll meet
The company below, then. I repeat,
The Count your master's known munificence
Is ample warrant that no just pretense   50
Of mine for dowry will be disallowed;
Though his fair daughter's self, as I avowed
At starting, is my object. Nay, we'll go
Together down, sir. Notice Neptune, though,
Taming a sea-horse, thought a rarity,   55
Which Claus of Innsbruck cast in bronze for me!

433. The first four lines of the poem contain all of the following
EXCEPT
(A) simile
(B) onomatopoeia
(C) masculine rhyme
(D) enjambment
(E) a caesura

434. The tone of the poem is primarily one of
(A) chilling aplomb
(B) wistful nostalgia
(C) aching self-pity
(D) suppressed grief
(E) sophisticated hauteur

435. The subject of the verb "read" in line 6 is
(A) Frà Pandolf
(B) pictured countenance
(C) glance
(D) strangers
(E) I

436. The form of the poem is a(n)
(A) Petrarchan sonnet
(B) villanelle
(C) dramatic monologue
(D) verse elegy
(E) epistle

437. The poet's attitude toward the duke is one of
(A) contempt
(B) pity
(C) admiration
(D) wariness
(E) envy

438. All of the following caused the duchess to blush EXCEPT
(A) "My favor at her breast" (line 25)
(B) "The dropping of the daylight in the West" (line 26)
(C) A "bough of cherries" (line 27)
(D) A "white mule / She rode with round the terrace" (lines 28–
29)
(E) A "nine-hundred-years-old name" (line 33)

439. The duchess's "looks went everywhere" (line 24) because she was
    (A) licentious
    (B) risible
    (C) vivacious
    (D) foolish
    (E) brazen

440. In line 36, the phrase "to make your will" most closely means to
    (A) write your last testament
    (B) make a will for the duchess
    (C) command the duchess
    (D) impose your desire
    (E) have a purpose

441. The duke's main complaint about his last duchess is most closely
    expressed in the line(s)
    (A) "'twas not / Her husband's presence only, called that spot /
        Of joy into the Duchess' cheek" (lines 13–15)
    (B) "she liked whate'er / She looked on" (line 23–24)
    (C) "[She] plainly set / Her wits to yours, forsooth, and made
        excuse" (lines 40–41)
    (D) "she smiled, no doubt, / Whene'er I passed her" (lines 43–44)
    (E) "all smiles stopped together" (line 46)

442. The sentence in lines 35–43 that begins "Even had you skill /
    In speech . . ." is an example of a(n)
    (A) extended metaphor
    (B) periodic sentence
    (C) run-on sentence
    (D) understatement
    (E) apostrophe

443. The word "munificence" in line 49 most closely means
    (A) affluence
    (B) prestige
    (C) influence
    (D) erudition
    (E) generosity

444. The word "warrant" in line 50 most closely means
    (A) bail
    (B) arraignment
    (C) proof
    (D) disclaimer
    (E) legal advice

445. The occasion for the poem seems to be a(n)
    (A) wedding
    (B) social visit
    (C) state dinner
    (D) marriage arrangement
    (E) art exposition

446. The phrases "Will't please you rise?" (line 47), "I repeat" (line 48),
     and "Nay, we'll go / Together down" (lines 53–54) indicate that
     (A) the count's envoy has attempted to leave the duke's presence
     (B) the duke has a strong sense of "noblesse oblige"
     (C) dinner has been served
     (D) the art exhibition is closing for the evening
     (E) the duke is in charge of the evening

447. The last three lines of the poem relate to the rest of the poem by
     (A) emphasizing the value of the duke's art collection
     (B) demonstrating the duke's pride in his art collection
     (C) revealing the duke's artistic sensibilities
     (D) confirming the duke's egotism
     (E) creating a connection between the duchess and the god
         Neptune

See page 134 for the answers to this set of questions.

Part I: Multiple-Choice Questions ❖ 117

READING 35: "LANDCRAB" BY MARGARET ATWOOD

QUESTIONS 448–458. Carefully read the poem before choosing your answers.

A lie, that we come from water.
The truth is we were born
from stones, dragons, the sea's
teeth, as you testify,[1]
with your crust and jagged scissors.   5

Hermit, hard socket
for a timid eye
you're a soft gut scuttling
sideways, a bone skull,
round bone on the prowl.   10
Wolf of treeroots and gravelly holes,
a mount on stilts,
the husk of a small demon.

Attack, voracious
eating, and flight: 15
it's a sound routine
for staying alive on edges.
Then there's the tide, and that dance
you do for the moon
on wet sand, claws raised   20
to fend off your mate,
your coupling a quick
dry clatter of rocks.
For mammals
with their lobes and bulbs,   25
scruples and warm milk,
you've nothing but contempt.

Here you are, a frozen scowl
targeted in flashlight,
then gone: a piece of what   30
we are, not all,
my stunted child, my momentary
face in the mirror,
My tiny nightmare.

448. The poem begins
(A) with an antithesis
(B) as a dramatic monologue
(C) with a personification
(D) in medias res
(E) with a colloquialism

---

[1] Allusion to two Greek myths about the creation of men (not women): Deucalion sowing stones and Cadmus sowing dragon's teeth.

449. The poem is unique in that it is told
    (A) by an unreliable narrator
    (B) in the present tense
    (C) in second person
    (D) without a narrator
    (E) from a personal point of view

450. The word "Hermit" in the second stanza (line 6) is a(n)
    (A) metaphor
    (B) hyperbole
    (C) literary conceit
    (D) didacticism
    (E) double entendre

451. The poem has a notable number of
    (A) similes
    (B) paired opposites
    (C) parallel structures
    (D) tercets
    (E) digressions

452. The word "sound" in line 16 most closely means
    (A) unreasonable
    (B) excessive
    (C) sensible
    (D) foolish
    (E) loud

453. All of the following lines could apply either to crabs or to humans EXCEPT
    (A) "we were born / from stones" (lines 2–3)
    (B) "Attack, voracious / eating, and flight" (lines 14–15)
    (C) "claws raised / to fend off your mate" (line 20–21)
    (D) "their lobes and bulbs" (line 25)
    (E) "a frozen scowl" (line 28)

454. The tone of the poem can best be described as one of
    (A) curious probing
    (B) mild revulsion
    (C) careful objectivity
    (D) playful grandiloquence
    (E) muted terror

455. Lines 22–23, "your coupling a quick / dry clatter of rocks," include
    (A) cacophony
    (B) internal rhyme
    (C) synesthesia
    (D) antonyms
    (E) eye rhyme

456. Lines 24–27, beginning "For mammals / with their lobes and bulbs," include
    (A) feminine rhyme
    (B) assonance
    (C) euphony
    (D) synecdoche
    (E) understatement

457. Which phrase in the poem pinpoints the location of the setting?
    (A) "treeroots and gravelly holes" (line 11)
    (B) "staying alive on edges" (line 17)
    (C) "Then there's the tide" (line 18)
    (D) "targeted in flashlight" (line 29)
    (E) "face in the mirror" (linc 33)

458. The poem moves from
    (A) assertion, to observation, to personal reflection
    (B) abstract idea, to concrete specifics, to revised abstract idea
    (C) metaphor, to description, to allusion
    (D) theory, to example, to application
    (E) crabs, to humans, to all mammals

See page 134 for the answers to this set of questions.

READING 36: EXCERPT FROM *HAMLET* BY WILLIAM SHAKESPEARE

Questions 459–470. Carefully read the passage, from Act 2, Scene 2, before choosing your answers.

HAMLET: . . . O, what a rogue and peasant slave am I!
Is it not monstrous that this player here,
But in a fiction, in a dream of passion,
Could force his soul so to his own conceit
That from her working all his visage wann'd,   5
Tears in his eyes, distraction in his aspect,
A broken voice, an' his whole function suiting
With forms to his conceit? And all for nothing,
For Hecuba?
What's Hecuba to him, or he to [Hecuba],   10
That he should weep for her? What would he do
Had he the motive and [the cue] for passion
That I have? He would drown the stage with tears,
And cleave the general ear with horrid speech,
Make mad the guilty, and appall the free,   15
Confound the ignorant, and amaze, indeed
The very faculties of eyes and ears. Yet I,
A dull and muddy-mettled rascal, peak
Like John-a-dreams, unpregnant of my cause,
And can say nothing; no, not for a king,   20
Upon whose property and most dear life
A damn'd defeat was made. Am I a coward?
Who calls me villain, breaks my pate across,
Plucks off my beard and blows it in my face,
Tweaks me by the nose, gives me the lie i' th' throat,   25
As deep as to the lungs. Who does me this?
Ha! 'swounds, I should take it: for it cannot be
But I am pigeon-liver'd, and lack gall
To make oppression bitter, or ere this
I should 'a' fatted all the region kites   30
With this slave's offal. Bloody, bawdy villain!
Remorseless, treacherous, lecherous, kindless villain!
Why, what an ass am I! This is most brave,
That I, the son of a dear [father] murthered,
Prompted to my revenge by heaven and hell,   35
Must like a whore unpack my heart with words,
And fall a-cursing like a very drab,
A stallion! Fie upon't, foh!
About, my brains! Hum—I have heard
That guilty creatures sitting at a play   40
Have by the very cunning of the scene
Been strook so to the soul, that presently
They have proclaim'd their malefactions:
For murther, though it have no tongue, will speak
With most miraculous organ. I'll have these players   45

Play something like the murther of my father
Before mine uncle: I'll observe his looks,
I'll tent him to the quick. If 'a do blench,
I know my course. The spirit that I have seen
May be a [dev'l], and the [dev'l] hath power   50
T' assume a pleasing shape, yea, and perhaps,
Out of my weakness and my melancholy,
As he is very potent with such spirits,
Abuses me to damn me. I'll have grounds
More relative than this—the play's the thing   55
Wherein I'll catch the conscience of the King.

459. This speech is spoken by one character directly to the audience.
It reveals thoughts and feelings that other characters are not
meant to hear. Such a speech, usually given when no one else is
present on stage, is called a(n)
(A) dramatic monologue
(B) metrical romance
(C) soliloquy
(D) sonnet
(E) epic simile

460. Hamlet calls himself a "rogue and peasant slave" (line 1) as he
compares himself with the actor because the actor
(A) was really not very good in acting this fiction
(B) feigned deep emotion
(C) chastised Hamlet
(D) reproached Hamlet's father
(E) castigated Hamlet's uncle

461. "He would drown the stage with tears" (line 13) is an example of
(A) hyperbole
(B) anaphora
(C) euphemism
(D) proscenium
(E) oxymoron

462. In the line "That from her working all his visage wann'd" (line 5),
"her" refers to
(A) the soul
(B) Hamlet
(C) the actor
(D) God
(E) Shakespeare

463. "For Hecuba? / What's Hecuba to him, or he to [Hecuba], / That
he should weep for her? What would he do / Had he the motive
and [the cue] for passion / That I have?" (lines 9–13) shows
Hamlet's questioning
(A) the actor's response
(B) his own response to his father's death
(C) Hecuba's response
(D) the value of actors and acting
(E) the meaning of life

464. The words "cleave the general ear with horrid speech, / . . . The very faculties of eyes and ears" (lines 14–17) show that Hamlet would like to
    (A) run away from the actor
    (B) kill the actor and then run away
    (C) muster the emotion shown by the actor
    (D) forget the actor
    (E) be like Hecuba

465. Hamlet declares, "Yet I, / A dull and muddy-mettled rascal, peak / Like John-a-dreams, unpregnant of my cause, / And can say nothing" (lines 17–20), meaning he
    (A) thinks he is the same as the actor
    (B) thinks he is better than the actor
    (C) thinks the actor has shown him up
    (D) hates the actor
    (E) wants to abolish acting

466. When Hamlet asks himself a series of questions—"Am I a coward? / Who calls me villain, breaks my pate across, / Plucks off my beard and blows it in my face, / Tweaks me by the nose, gives me the lie i' th' throat, / As deep as to the lungs. Who does me this?" (lines 22–26)—he is using the time-honored
    (A) open-ended question
    (B) rhetorical question
    (C) closed question
    (D) question that was answered earlier
    (E) repetition of the same question

467. Hamlet believes that he is "pigeon-liver'd, and lack[s] gall" (line 28) and that he should have "fatted all the region kites / With this slave's offal" (lines 30–31) because
    (A) the actor deserves to die
    (B) the bloody villain deserves to die
    (C) Hamlet himself deserves to die
    (D) no one deserves to die
    (E) death, like offal, is just too awful

468. Hamlet refers to himself as an "ass" because he is "the son of a dear [father] murthered, / Prompted to my revenge by heaven and hell, / Must like a whore unpack my heart with words, / And fall a-cursing like a very drab, / A stallion" (lines 34–38). Hamlet thinks
    (A) his words without deeds have turned him into a harlot
    (B) he will easily get revenge
    (C) he will forget about revenge
    (D) his actions thus far have made an impact
    (E) he will be prompted to unpack from his recent trip

469. When Hamlet thinks of the soon-to-be-performed play, he
    (A) hates the thought of sitting through it because it will be tedious
    (B) thinks of getting the king to admit his wrongdoing
    (C) sends for a scullion
    (D) starts to memorize his lines for the play
    (E) thinks of his girlfriend

470. In the lines "I'll observe <u>his</u> looks, / I'll tent <u>him</u> to the quick. If <u>a'</u>
     <u>do</u> blench, / I know my course" (47–49), the underlined pronouns
     refer to
     (A) the actor
     (B) Hecuba
     (C) Hamlet's uncle
     (D) Hamlet's father
     (E) John-a-dreams

See page 135 for the answers to this set of questions.

READING 37: "SPINSTER" BY SYLVIA PLATH

QUESTIONS 471–485. Carefully read the poem before choosing your answers.

Now this particular girl
During a ceremonious April walk
With her latest suitor
Found herself, of a sudden, intolerably struck
By the birds' irregular babel 　　　　　　　　　5
And the leaves' litter.

By this tumult afflicted, she
Observed her lover's gestures unbalance the air,
His gait stray uneven
Through a rank wilderness of fern and flower. 　　10
She judged petals in disarray,
The whole season, sloven.

How she longed for winter then!—
Scrupulously austere in its order
Of white and black 　　　　　　　　　　　　15
Ice and rock, each sentiment within border,
And heart's frosty discipline
Exact as a snowflake.

But here—a burgeoning
Unruly enough to pitch her five queenly wits 　20
Into vulgar motley—
A treason not to be borne. Let idiots
Reel giddy in bedlam spring:
She withdrew neatly.

And round her house she set 　　　　　　　　25
Such a barricade of barb and check
Against mutinous weather
As no mere insurgent man could hope to break
With curse, fist, threat
Or love, either. 　　　　　　　　　　　　　30

471. The phrase "this particular girl" (line 1) is a(n)
    (A) oxymoron
    (B) double entendre
    (C) allusion
    (D) colloquialism
    (E) homonym

472. Which of the following pairs rhyme?
    I. particular girl (line 1) and irregular babel (line 5)
    II. suitor (line 3) and litter (line 6)
    III. winter then (line 13) and discipline (line 17)
    IV. motley (line 21) and spring (line 23)
    (A) I, II, and III only
    (B) I, II, and IV only
    (C) I, III, and IV only
    (D) I and IV only
    (E) II, III, and IV only

473. The poem's rhymes and rhythms reflect its theme of
    (A) courting and love
    (B) spring and summer
    (C) order and disorder
    (D) connection and isolation
    (E) austerity and gaiety

474. The poem includes all of the following EXCEPT
    (A) alliteration
    (B) assonance
    (C) slant rhyme
    (D) caesura
    (E) internal rhyme

475. The "five queenly wits" (line 20) are the girl's
    (A) friends
    (B) jesters
    (C) senses
    (D) suitors
    (E) jokes

476. The "tumult afflicted" (line 7) refers to
    (A) sorrow
    (B) the suitor
    (C) spring
    (D) an injury
    (E) an insult

477. In several places, the diction alludes to
    (A) marriage
    (B) game-playing
    (C) hunting
    (D) warfare
    (E) court and the law

478. The tone is
    (A) aloof
    (B) disdainful
    (C) reverential
    (D) insinuating
    (E) compassionate

479. The phrase "unbalance the air" (line 8) indicates
    (A) the girl's disapproval
    (B) the lovers' dissonance with nature
    (C) a violent physical movement
    (D) Nature's disapproval of the pair
    (E) the suitor's disruption of nature's harmony

480. As used here, the word "rank" (line 10) most closely means
    (A) eminent
    (B) blatant
    (C) fetid
    (D) profuse
    (E) brazen

481. The consonants in lines 3, 5, 12, and 17 are
    (A) consonant
    (B) palindromatic
    (C) onomatopoetic
    (D) assonant
    (E) homilic

482. The poem is a
    (A) complaint
    (B) lament
    (C) justification
    (D) requiem
    (E) plea

483. The "spinster" of the title lives within a
    (A) citadel of solitude
    (B) lovers' hideaway
    (C) fortress armed against calamity
    (D) stronghold of passion
    (E) castle under siege

484. The word "bedlam" (line 23) shares a connotation with the word
    (A) burgeoning (line 19)
    (B) queenly (line 20)
    (C) motley (line 21)
    (D) treason (line 22)
    (E) idiots (line 22)

485. The word "insurgent" as used in line 28 means
    (A) boorish
    (B) irritating
    (C) innocuous
    (D) ungovernable
    (E) invidious

See page 135 for the answers to this set of questions.

READING 38: "OZYMANDIAS" BY PERCY BYSSHE SHELLEY

QUESTIONS 486–500. Carefully read the poem before choosing your answers.

> I met a traveler from an antique land
> Who said: Two vast and trunkless legs of stone
> Stand in the desert . . . Near them, on the sand,
> Half sunk, a shattered visage lies, whose frown,
> And wrinkled lip, and sneer of cold command   5
> Tell that its sculptor well those passions read
> Which yet survive, stamped on these lifeless things,
> The hand that mocked them, and the heart that fed;
> And on the pedestal these words appear:
> "My name is Ozymandias, king of kings;   10
> Look on my works, ye Mighty, and despair!"
> Nothing beside remains. Round the decay
> Of that colossal wreck, boundless and bare
> The lone and level sands stretch far away.

486. The objects in the first stanza are significant for their
    (A) antiquity
    (B) composition
    (C) dismemberment
    (D) succession
    (E) magnitude

487 The meter of the poem is
    (A) iambic tetrameter
    (B) iambic pentameter
    (C) trochaic dimeter
    (D) spondaic trimeter
    (E) alexandrine

488. The poem contains
    (A) slant rhyme
    (B) feminine rhyme
    (C) internal rhyme
    (D) rime riche
    (E) assonance

489. The poem includes all of the following EXCEPT a(n)
    (A) octave
    (B) sestet
    (C) couplet
    (D) turn
    (E) tercet

490. The poem is
    (A) exhortatory
    (B) idyllic
    (C) funereal
    (D) ironic
    (E) pastoral

491. There is a mood shift in the poem after line
    (A) 8
    (B) 9
    (C) 10
    (D) 13
    (E) 14

492. The "hand" and "heart" referred to in line 8 belong to
    (A) the poet
    (B) the narrator
    (C) Ozymandias
    (D) travelers
    (E) the sculptor

493. The word "heart" in line 8 acts as a
    (A) synecdoche
    (B) metonymy
    (C) synesthesia
    (D) double entendre
    (E) motif

494. All of the following themes appear in the poem EXCEPT
    (A) the power of the artist
    (B) despair of the mighty
    (C) the folly of ignorance
    (D) the impermanence of human endeavor
    (E) the inevitability of decay

495. The word "stamped" (line 7) does all of the following EXCEPT
    (A) serves as the verb of the sentence
    (B) has three direct objects
    (C) modifies passions
    (D) alliterates with an adjective clause
    (E) provides a key to understanding the poem

496. The subject of the last sentence in the poem is
    (A) round
    (B) decay
    (C) wreck
    (D) lone
    (E) sands

497. Most of the diction is
    (A) Anglo-Saxon
    (B) Latinate
    (C) elevated
    (D) erudite
    (E) somber

498. The last stanza
    (A) underscores the previous stanza
    (B) symbolizes eternity
    (C) exemplifies verisimilitude
    (D) alludes to Ozymandias's downfall
    (E) is an objective correlative

499. The main irony of the poem is found in lines
    (A) 3–5
    (B) 6
    (C) 7–8
    (D) 10–12
    (E) 12–13

500. In the poem, who or what gets the final word?
    (A) the narrator
    (B) the traveler
    (C) time
    (D) Ozymandias
    (E) the sculptor

See page 135 for the answers to this set of questions.

ANSWERS FOR THE MULTIPLE-CHOICE QUESTIONS IN PART I

READING 1: EXCERPT FROM "THE LOTTERY" BY SHIRLEY JACKSON

1. A	2. E	3. B	4. E	5. C
6. C	7. C	8. A	9. E	10. C
11. A	12. E	13. E	14. E	

READING 2: "SAILING TO BYZANTIUM" BY WILLIAM BUTLER YEATS

15. D	16. A	17. D	18. E	19. D
20. A	21. E	22. C	23. A	24. E
25. B	26. A	27. B	28. C	29. C

READING 3: "THE DEATH OF THE BALL TURRET GUNNER" BY RANDALL JARRELL

30. D	31. A	32. D	33. D	34. D
35. E	36. D	37. A	38. E	39. E
40. A	41. C			

READING 4: EXCERPT FROM *TRYING TO FIND CHINATOWN* BY DAVID HENRY HWANG

42. B	43. C	44. B	45. B	46. E
47. E	48. D	49. E	50. A	51. D
52. D	53. A	54. E		

READING 5: "IMAGINE" BY JOHN LENNON

55. E	56. C	57. B	58. A	59. B
60. E	61. D	62. A	63. C	64. D
65. A	66. C	67. D		

READING 6: "CINDERELLA" BY ANNE SEXTON

68. C	69. A	70. E	71. E	72. A
73. D	74. B	75. D	76. E	77. C
78. B	79. A			

READING 7: "A VALEDICTION: FORBIDDING MOURNING" BY JOHN DONNE

80. B	81. C	82. D	83. C	84. A
85. B	86. C	87. B	88. D	89. C
90. D	91. B	92. A	93. B	94. A

READING 8: "LOST SISTER" BY CATHY SONG

95. A	96. B	97. B	98. C	99. B
100. C	101. D	102. A	103. E	104. C
105. C	106. A			

READING 9: "CHRIST CLIMBED DOWN" BY LAWRENCE FERLINGHETTI

107. B	108. A	109. D	110. A	111. D
112. A	113. B	114. E	115. B	116. D
117. A	118. C	119. B	120. B	121. C

READING 10: EXCERPT FROM *A MIDSUMMER NIGHT'S DREAM* BY WILLIAM SHAKESPEARE

122. B	123. B	124. D	125. C	126. A
127. D	128. C	129. B	130. D	131. E
132. A	133. A	134. C	135. B	136. E

READING 11: EXCERPT FROM "THE CASK OF AMONTILLADO" BY EDGAR ALLAN POE

137. C	138. B	139. C	140. A	141. B
142. A	143. D	144. A	145. C	146. E
147. A	148. E	149. A	150. E	151. C

READING 12: "DADDY" BY SYLVIA PLATH

152. D	153. A	154. B	155. C	156. D
157. B	158. A	159. E	160. C	161. D
162. B	163. E			

READING 13: "ARS POETICA" BY ARCHIBALD MACLEISH

164. B	165. C	166. A	167. D	168. A
169. C	170. B	171. A	172. E	173. C
174. A	175. B	176. B	177. A	

READING 14: "TO THE VIRGINS, TO MAKE MUCH OF TIME" BY ROBERT HERRICK

178. D	179. A	180. C	181. B	182. D
183. A	184. D	185. A	186. C	187. E
188. E				

READING 15: EXCERPT FROM *DEATH OF A SALESMAN* BY ARTHUR MILLER

189. D	190. A	191. C	192. B	193. A
194. B	195. C	196. E	197. B	198. D
199. C	200. A	201. C	202. C	203. B

READING 16: "MAIN CHARACTER" BY JIMMY SANTIAGO BACA

204. C	205. A	206. C	207. E	208. D
209. B	210. A	211. C	212. B	213. D
214. E	215. C	216. D		

READING 17: EXCERPT FROM *OEDIPUS REX* BY SOPHOCLES

217. C	218. B	219. A	220. D	221. B
222. A	223. B	224. A	225. A	226. B

READING 18: EXCERPT FROM "CATHEDRAL" BY RAYMOND CARVER

227. D	228. A	229. E	230. C	231. B
232. C	233. E	234. D	235. B	236. E

READING 19: "KUBLA KHAN, OR, A VISION IN A DREAM. A FRAGMENT" BY SAMUEL TAYLOR COLERIDGE

237. C	238. D	239. A	240. B	241. B
242. E	243. A	244. A	245. B	246. C
247. B	248. D	249. D		

READING 20: "THE PLOT" BY JORGE LUIS BORGES

250. B	251. B	252. A	253. D	254. A
255. E	256. B	257. E	258. C	259. A

READING 21: "HOW DO I LOVE THEE?" BY ELIZABETH BARRETT BROWNING

260. B	261. D	262. D	263. A	264. B
265. A	266. C	267. D	268. E	269. E
270. E	271. E	272. B	273. B	274. C

READING 22: EXCERPT FROM *THE SANDBOX* BY EDWARD ALBEE

275. A	276. C	277. A	278. B	279. C
280. C	281. D	282. A	283. B	284. E
285. D	286. B	287. A	288. C	289. E

READING 23: "TO HIS COY MISTRESS" BY ANDREW MARVELL

290. D	291. C	292. D	293. E	294. B
295. D	296. A	297. B	298. B	299. E

READING 24: "DO NOT GO GENTLE INTO THAT GOOD NIGHT" BY DYLAN THOMAS

300. D	301. A	302. C	303. B	304. D
305. A	306. D	307. B	308. D	309. A
310. B	311. C	312. D	313. A	314. C

READING 25: "A SUPERMARKET IN CALIFORNIA" BY ALLEN GINSBERG

315. D	316. A	317. E	318. B	319. C
320. E	321. A	322. E	323. A	324. A
325. D				

READING 26: "THAT TIME OF YEAR THOU MAYST IN ME BEHOLD" BY WILLIAM SHAKESPEARE

326. D	327. B	328. D	329. A	330. C
331. B	332. C	333. B	334. A	335. C
336. E	337. A	338. B	339. B	

READING 27: "GOD'S GRANDEUR" BY GERARD MANLEY HOPKINS

340. C	341. A	342. B	343. B	344. C
345. E	346. B	347. D	348. D	349. B
350. A	351. D	352. C	353. A	354. B

READING 28: "MID-TERM BREAK" BY SEAMUS HEANEY

355. B	356. A	357. C	358. E	359. C
360. A	361. D	362. D	363. C	364. C
365. C	366. E	367. A		

READING 29: "BATTER MY HEART, THREE-PERSONED GOD" BY JOHN DONNE

368. B	369. D	370. E	371. C	372. A
373. B	374. E	375. C	376. C	377. B
378. D	379. E	380. D	381. D	382. A

READING 30: "AMERICA" BY CLAUDE MCKAY

383. E	384. A	385. C	386. D	387. B
388. C	389. B	390. B	391. D	392. A
393. B				

READING 31: "THE CLOD AND THE PEBBLE" BY WILLIAM BLAKE

394. A	395. B	396. C	397. D	398. D
399. E	400. B	401. B	402. C	403. B
404. D	405. B	406. B	407. A	

READING 32: "MEN AT FORTY" BY DONALD JUSTICE

408. E	409. A	410. C	411. A	412. D
413. B	414. E	415. E	416. A	417. B
418. C				

READING 33: EXCERPT FROM "BARTLEBY THE SCRIVENER: A STORY OF WALL STREET" BY HERMAN MELVILLE

419. E	420. B	421. B	422. C	423. C
424. B	425. D	426. B	427. A	428. A
429. C	430. B	431. E	432. C	

READING 34: "MY LAST DUCHESS" BY ROBERT BROWNING

433. B	434. A	435. D	436. C	437. A
438. A	439. C	440. D	441. A	442. B
443. E	444. C	445. D	446. A	447. D

READING 35: "LANDCRAB" BY MARGARET ATWOOD

448. D	449. C	450. E	451. B	452. C
453. D	454. B	455. A	456. C	457. D
458. A				

READING 36: EXCERPT FROM *HAMLET* BY WILLIAM SHAKESPEARE

459. C	460. B	461. A	462. A	463. B
464. C	465. C	466. B	467. B	468. A
469. B	470. C			

READING 37: "SPINSTER" BY SYLVIA PLATH

471. B	472. A	473. C	474. E	475. C
476. C	477. E	478. A	479. A	480. D
481. B	482. C	483. A	484. E	485. D

READING 38: "OZYMANDIAS" BY PERCY BYSSHE SHELLEY

486. C	487. A	488. A	489. C	490. D
491. A	492. E	493. A	494. B	495. A
496. E	497. A	498. B	499. D	500. C

Part II

Essay Questions

QUESTION 1: ON "THEME FOR ENGLISH B" BY LANGSTON HUGHES AND "INTRODUCTION TO POETRY" BY BILLY COLLINS

In the two poems below, Langston Hughes and Billy Collins write about creative experiences. Carefully read the poems, then write an essay in which you apply Collins's rules of interpretation to Hughes's poem. In your essay, consider such elements as figurative language, versification, tone, and theme.

Theme for English B
by Langston Hughes

The instructor said,

Go home, and write
a page tonight.
And let that page come out of you—
Then, it will be true.   5

I wonder if it's that simple?
I am twenty-two, colored, born in Winston-Salem.
I went to school there, then Durham, then here
to this college on the hill above Harlem.
I am the only colored student in my class.   10
The steps from the hill lead down into Harlem,
through a park, then I cross St. Nicholas,
Eighth Avenue, Seventh, and I come to the Y,
the Harlem Branch Y, where I take the elevator
up to my room, sit down, and write this page: 15

It's not easy to know what is true for you or me
at twenty-two, my age. But I guess I'm what
I feel and see and hear, Harlem, I hear you:
hear you, hear me—we two—you, me, talk on this page.
(I hear New York too.) Me—who?   20

Well, I like to eat, sleep, drink, and be in love.
I like to work, read, learn, and understand life.
I like a pipe for a Christmas present,
or records—Bessie, bop, or Bach.
I guess being colored doesn't make me *not* like   25
the same things other folks like who are other races.
So will my page be colored that I write?
Being me, it will not be white.
But it will be
a part of you, instructor.   30
You are white—
yet a part of me, as I am a part of you.
That's American.
Sometimes perhaps you don't want to be a part of me.
Nor do I often want to be a part of you.   35
But we are, that's true!
As I learn from you,

I guess you learn from me—
although you're older—and white—
and somewhat more free.   40

This is my page for English B.

Introduction to Poetry
by Billy Collins

I ask them to take a poem
and hold it up to the light
like a color slide

or press an ear against its hive.

I say drop a mouse into a poem   5
and watch him probe his way out,

or walk inside the poem's room
and feel the walls for a light switch.

I want them to waterski
across the surface of a poem   10
waving at the author's name on the shore.

But all they want to do
is tie the poem to a chair with rope
and torture a confession out of it.

They begin beating it with a hose   15
to find out what it really means.

SAMPLE ESSAY 1

Billy Collins writes a poem about how to properly analyze a poem. In this "how to" approach he uses creative imagery and metaphors. He seems to suggest that analysis of poetry should be a simple and enjoyable act like holding it up to the light or like listening to it as you would a beehive. He strongly disapproves of any forceful interpretation and compares that type of analysis to beating the poem up in order to get the truth out of it. Collins uses his poem's figurative language to tell the reader what he thinks. He suggests that readers will understand more clearly if they put themselves into the experience. When readers are placed in that situation they will be able to see the poem in very new ways as they examine other possible meanings and interpretations.

Collins's suggestions for analyzing the creative experience of poetry can be properly put to use with Langston Hughes's poem "Theme for English B." Hughes uses as his subject a writing assignment for his English class. The prompt that Hughes needs to address for his assignment is to write something about yourself that is true and from deep within. That prompt is reminiscent of the Collins requirements.

Hughes will experience a writing that reveals an understanding of himself.

Hughes begins to write a poem that begins simply enough, with him explaining himself to another person. He names his place of birth, his school, and where he lives. He then ranges into imagery. He talks so we can hear Harlem and New York. They are indeed his home and are part of him. They influenced much of everything he says about himself. He lists what he likes, the basic human needs such as eating, sleeping, and loving. These things are a statement that he believes he is exactly like everyone else around him even though his race is different. The reader can use the suggestions of Collins and see the position and opinion on Hughes in his "Theme for English B" poem. The Hughes poem relates to all of us. Just because Hughes is a person of color, his words on the paper are still truly him.

The techniques suggested by Billy Collins are a great method for explaining any poems. The poem by Hughes emphasizes the true connectivity of all humans when they are creative. As Collins suggests, when we experience a poem and place ourselves in the poem, we must do it slowly and with patience, not harshly and brutally. We must get a sense of the poem, not torture a confession out of it. We must ski over the top of each line, leaving full understanding in the synesthesia of our wake. We must follow the mouse of skepticism through the maze of ideas. We must feel around in the darkness of uncertainty and learn that we do not need to turn on the spotlight of complete knowledge. Collins points out that the reader should not get frustrated when meaning is not apparent. It is only then, as Collins suggests, that we will find the truth and understanding and attempt answers that approach and often get at the real meaning of the poem. We must avoid the usual heavy-handed approach many students take. As Collins suggests, a heavy-handed analysis usually destroys the essence of poetry, the light, the sound, the air, the sheer beauty filtered through words. Insights into the poem about the creative process used by Hughes when he was writing a theme for his college English class can be so much better when held to the process suggested by Collins. The best method to use shows a deep explanation that lends itself to the easygoing precision of the steps in an explication suggested by Collins.

COMMENT ON SAMPLE ESSAY 1

This essay makes many specific references to both poems with ideas that are cogent, free of plot summary, and relevant to the prompt. The essay is not without minor flaws, but overall it demonstrates the writer's ability to discuss the poems with some degree of insight and understanding. It is focused on the prompt, and provides specific support for detecting the overall meaning of both poems. For the most part, the essay is well written, although there is some immaturity and lack of control in places.

SAMPLE ESSAY 2

In the poem "Introduction to Poetry," Billy Collins gives the reader a basis for how poetry should be read and analyzed. The guidelines he gives correspond with the Hughes poem, and with Collins's guidelines as a tool one can understand the poetic imagery, structure, and meaning in the way the author intended.

In the first stanza of "Introduction to Poetry" Collins uses the word "color" as a description of the mood and personality of the poem by holding it "up to the light." Hughes also references "color" in his "Theme for English B." Hughes is referring to the color of skin. The great contrast between the two meanings of the same word allows the reader to interpret the Hughes poem using color to describe himself because everyone around him assumes that color defines his personality because of the fact that he is "of color."

Collins points out that a reader of poetry can "press an ear against the hive," because a poem has a lot more meaning behind it. "Theme for English B" could be looked at as merely a simple assignment by Hughes to talk about his life, but it is also poetic in every respect. This poem has a stanza structure that adds to the piece. It also has rhyme and makes many allusions to places in Harlem and recordings of the time.

Collins uses figurative language such as personification, while Hughes uses colors. While Hughes dwells on racial stereotypes, Collins tells us to not get frustrated when a poem's meaning is not as apparent as we would want it to be.

To get to know what the poetry of Hughes is all about, the reader must find what he is feeling and get at the tone of the work. I think that the tone points out a type of sarcastic ignorance because Hughes battled prejudice for his entire life. In conclusion, Collins gives guidelines that allow the reader to go beyond the surface to get at the true meaning.

COMMENT ON SAMPLE ESSAY 2

This essay is superficial. The discussion of meaning in both poems is a tad formulaic and mechanical, and is inadequately related to the chosen details. The essay reveals naïve thinking and writing and exhibits inconsistent control over the elements of composition. It is not well organized or developed, but the writing is sufficient in most areas to convey the writer's ideas. The contentions in certain areas are on target, but more frequently are flimsy, imprecise, and ineffective.

QUESTION 2: ON "THE FISH" BY ELIZABETH BISHOP

Carefully read Elizabeth Bishop's poem "The Fish." Then write an essay in which you describe how the speaker's attitude toward the fish in lines 1–46 is related to her attitude toward it in lines 47–64. Using specific references to the text, show how such aspects as verse form, language, and tone contribute to the reader's understanding of those attitudes.

I caught a tremendous fish
and held him beside the boat
half out of water, with my hook
fast in a corner of his mouth.
He didn't fight.   5
He hadn't fought at all.
He hung a grunting weight,
battered and venerable
and homely. Here and there
his brown skin hung in strips   10
like ancient wallpaper,
and its pattern of darker brown
was like wallpaper:
shapes like full-blown roses
stained and lost through age.   15
He was speckled with barnacles,
fine rosettes of lime,
and infested
with tiny white sea-lice,
and underneath two or three   20
rags of green weed hung down.
While his gills were breathing in
the terrible oxygen
—the frightening gills,
fresh and crisp with blood,   25
that can cut so badly—
I thought of the coarse white flesh
packed in like feathers,
the big bones and the little bones,
the dramatic reds and blacks   30
of his shiny entrails,
and the pink swim-bladder
like a big peony.
I looked into his eyes
which were far larger than mine   35
but shallower, and yellowed,
the irises backed and packed
with tarnished tinfoil
seen through the lenses
of old scratched isinglass.   40
They shifted a little, but not
to return my stare.
—It was more like the tipping

of an object toward the light.
I admired his sullen face,   45
the mechanism of his jaw,
and then I saw
that from his lower lip
—if you could call it a lip—
grim, wet, and weaponlike,   50
hung five old pieces of fish-line,
or four and a wire leader
with the swivel still attached,
with all their five big hooks
grown firmly in his mouth.   55
A green line, frayed at the end
where he broke it, two heavier lines,
and a fine black thread
still crimped from the strain and snap
when it broke and he got away.   60
Like medals with their ribbons
frayed and wavering,
a five-haired beard of wisdom
trailing from his aching jaw.
I stared and stared   65
and victory filled up
the little rented boat,
from the pool of bilge
where oil had spread a rainbow
around the rusted engine   70
to the bailer rusted orange,
the sun-cracked thwarts,
the oarlocks on their strings,
the gunnels—until everything
was rainbow, rainbow, rainbow!   75
And I let the fish go.

SAMPLE ESSAY 1

In the poem "The Fish," the narrator's attitude toward the fish changes from one of intrigued interest to respect and a sense of shared victory, transforming this seemingly dead and nameless creature into a living, fighting, and breathing wonder.

The author's first adjective to describe the fish as "tremendous" (1) reveals to the reader that the narrator feels immensely proud of her catch. However, right away a note of puzzlement creeps in, for the narrator states, "He didn't fight. / He hadn't fought at all" (5-6). Intrigued by uncertainty, the narrator goes probing for the answer. She describes every intimate detail of the fish in vivid detail and utilizes colors extensively, starting with bland ones like "brown" and progressing to brighter ones like "reds and blacks," "pink," and "yellow" (10, 30, 32, 36). In the first part of the poem, she compares the "strips" of "brown skin" to "wallpaper" shaped like "full-blown roses" (10, 14), transforming its skin from bland brownness into something dainty and refined. She finds the fish strangely beautiful, but she describes it in the same way a painter would describe a work conducted as a still life: an immobile object that is perfectly attuned to the artist's liking. This method allows for the artist to be in total control, without having to worry about her subject interfering. But something about the fish does interfere, for in an attempt to understand the fish the narrator even gazed into the fish's almost inanimate eyes, with their "irises backed and packed / with tarnished tinfoil," in hopes of enlightenment (37–38). The gaze the fish returns hold no answers, however.

Then the narrator notices the fish's lower lip and her attitude begins to change. She sees in the fish's mouth five big hooks that all belonged to other fishermen that the fish had defeated. The narrator describes the hooks and dangling lines with growing respect for the fish, comparing them to "medals with their ribbons" and asserting that the fish had a "five-haired beard of wisdom" (61 & 63). The narrator now realizes that she has succeeded where many past fishermen have failed and she swells with victory. In the author's moment of victory she decides to let the fish go in the hope that more people will have the opportunity to catch the fish. The colors that are woven throughout the poem now converge into Nature's sign of victory: the rainbow.

COMMENT ON SAMPLE ESSAY 1

This very successful essay, written in a bold, compelling style, demonstrates a clear understanding of both the poem and the prompt. It is convincing and original, and it avoids mere summary or paraphrasing. It includes an impressive range of specific details that are discussed with perception.

SAMPLE ESSAY 2

The poem, "The Fish," describes a fish that is caught and held captive while the fisherman makes various observations about the fish. Through these observations, the reader is witness to the change in attitude the narrator displays for the fish.

The beginning of the poem, specifically lines 1–46, shows that the fisherman has only disgust for the fish. The narrator claims that "he didn't fight" (5) and that "he hung a grunting weight, battered and venerable and homely" (7–9). It seems as though the narrator is almost unhappy with his catch, as though the fish owed him more entertainment than he had provided. The narrator recognizes that the fish is ugly and must be very old. He goes on to comment on the pure unpleasantness of the fish's appearance, how it is "speckled with barnacles . . . and infested with tiny white sea-lice" (16–19). The narrator continues in his berating of the fish throughout most of the poem.

But his attitude toward the fish clearly changes in line 47, "and then I saw." The line is intentionally shorter than all the rest, drawing attention to itself. The narrator now sees the fish in a different way.

His earlier disgust for the fish now seems outdated. The fish has some pieces of fishing line hanging from its lip, from which "hung five old pieces of fish-line, / or four and a wire leader / with the swivel still attached, / with all their five big hooks / grown firmly in his mouth . . . medals with their ribbons /frayed and wavering, /a five-haired beard of wisdom" (51–64). The narrator's tone goes from disgust to admiration because of this one observation.

The narrator's differing tones also show a change from disgust to a better view. In other words, the narrator's disgust was merely an uninformed view of the creature. The discovery of the fish-lines makes the narrator have a new view of the fish and gives both the narrator and the reader a new way to view fish in general.

COMMENT ON SAMPLE ESSAY 2
The opening of this essay basically repeats the prompt without demonstrating an understanding of either the prompt or the poem. It does not develop ideas in depth. Instead, the student gives a mere listing of what the poet does, with little or no original thought—actually misinterpreting some lines. The writing is adequate, but not sophisticated.

QUESTION 3: ON "THE PASSIONATE SHEPHERD TO HIS LOVE" BY CHRISTOPHER MARLOWE AND "THE NYMPH'S REPLY TO THE SHEPHERD" BY SIR WALTER RALEIGH

In each of the following poems, the speaker presents a view of life and of love. Carefully read the poems. Then write an essay in which you compare and contrast the two poems, analyzing the poetic techniques each writer uses to present his views.

The Passionate Shepherd to His Love
by Christopher Marlowe

Come live with me and be my love,
And we will all the pleasures prove
That valleys, groves, hills, and fields,
Woods, or steepy mountain yields.

And we will sit upon the rocks,   5
Seeing the shepherds feed their flocks
By shallow rivers, to whose falls
Melodious birds sing madrigals.

And I will make thee beds of roses
And a thousand fragrant posies,   10
A cap of flowers and a kirtle
Embroidered all with leaves of myrtle;

A gown made of the finest wool
Which from our pretty lambs we pull;
Fair-linèd slippers for the cold,   15
With buckles of the purest gold;

A belt of straw and ivy buds,
With coral clasps and amber studs.
And if these pleasures may thee move,
Come live with me and be my love.   20

The shepherds' swains shall dance and sing
For thy delight each May morning.
If these delights thy mind may move,
Then live with me and be my love.

The Nymph's Reply to the Shepherd
by Sir Walter Raleigh

If all the world and love were young,
And truth in every shepherd's tongue,
These pretty pleasures might me move
To live with thee and be thy love.

Time drives the flocks from field to fold,   5
When rivers rage and rocks grow cold;
And Philomel becometh dumb;
The rest complains of cares to come.

The flowers do fade, and wanton fields
To wayward winter reckoning yields: 10
A honey tongue, a heart of gall,
Is fancy's spring, but sorrow's fall.

Thy gowns, thy shoes, thy beds of roses,
Thy cap, thy kirtle, and thy posies
Soon break, soon wither, soon forgotten,   15
In folly ripe, in reason rotten.

Thy belt of straw and ivy buds,
Thy coral clasps and amber studs,
All these in me no means can move
To come to thee and be thy love.   20

But could youth last, and love still breed,
Had joys no date, nor age no need,
Then these delights my mind might move
To live with thee and be thy love.

Sample Essay 1

The way we look at life often colors the way we look at love. These poems present different views of love in the world and place each under a distinct microscope. One takes the view of the head-in-the-clouds romantic while the other wears reality as a mocking badge of honor. In Christopher Marlowe's poem, "The Passionate Shepherd to His Love," the shepherd voices an opinion of love in a question-and-answer format. Sir Walter Raleigh, in a similar format, gives a mocking response to the shepherd's questions. Raleigh's poem, "The Nymph's Reply," gives answers that betray a view that asserts the coldness of the real world. The shepherd and the nymph look at life in two very different ways. Their views on life and love tell the reader that they inhabit two different worlds. The poems greatly contradict one another and each in its own way reveals love to be a positive attribute and a hidden evil.

As the shepherd speaks, it appears as though he is interested only in a very young and very impractical search for a mate that borders on the worst aspects of mere infatuation. He is very innocent and very hopeful in his search. He believes that he will find what he thinks is "true love." Many of the ideas and images that he provides are colorful and beautiful. They spring from his view of the world that believes that love can conquer the world's ills. He presents the world of his love as a Garden of Eden, a true paradise. The shepherd is a true romantic with very high and lofty expectations. He describes the clothing that will be worn by each of them. He imagines them wearing a fine and precious mixture of things from nature. He lists "fragrant posies" (line 10) and "Embroidered all with leaves of myrtle" (line 12). His view is brimming with only the good appearances of a pleasure-filled nature: flowers, lambs wool and fur-lined slippers. The jewels are ivory, coral and amber. His seasons are the never-ending summer and spring. He concludes his thoughts by saying that he and his lover will live always in harmony with one another. He speaks of perfection.

The nymph's reply to the shepherd, on the other hand, is quite the exact opposite. The nymph believes that love does not, and cannot, exist solely in the realm of romance. This highly idealized notion is merely disguised. The nymph knows that flattering youthfulness and strength will eventually fade, and that the world is real. The nymph is very pessimistic. She is playful and caustic as she mocks each of the shepherd's opinions. She views the so-called love expressed by the shepherd as sorely lacking and in need of a good dose of reality. She uses the same nature-laden images that he used. Only this time "the flowers do fade," (line 9) and "to wayward winter reckoning yields" (line 10). The nymph uses imagery from the real world filled with things that would be depressing and morbid to the shepherd. The nymph concludes her poem by saying that if youth could last forever, then so, too, could love. This phrase literally "spits in the face" of the hopeless romantic who believes that love lasts forever without difficulty.

The two poems are written in the exact same form, and the two portrayals of the idea of love could not be more different from one another. In fact, it is the parallel structure that draws attention to the differences. The "question-and-answer" style works well. The shepherd's questions seem rhetorical and the nymph's answers are brutally honest. Much can be learned from the nymph's depressing and dreadful responses. Perhaps the nymph has seen many lovers fall for one another and they end so tragically as time goes on. It is the nymph's experience that makes her wise, and the shepherd's innocence that allows him to be so ignorant of the world's ways.

COMMENT ON SAMPLE ESSAY 1

This essay offers a reasonable comparison and contrast of the two poems and an effective analysis of the relationship between them. While not without flaws, the discussion of the themes and techniques and the analysis of the relationship between the two poems is convincing.

SAMPLE ESSAY 2

In the two poems, "Passionate Shepherd" and "Nymph's Reply," we are ushered into two worlds of hopeless romantics. While expressing a desire for love, it comes with specific requirements that must be adhered to; otherwise the love in their minds would not exist.

In "The Passionate Shepherd to His Love" the narrator, presumably the shepherd himself, describes a sort of fairy-tale wonderland comparable to Eden's garden. This poem has a decidedly hopeful and eager tone as a result of attempting to convince his lady to be with him. The nature imagery and nature allusions to spring suggest that the narrator believes that love can conquer the world's sorrow and perhaps all evil. He believes that his love will really last forever and that it will create a paradise on earth. These beliefs add, I think, to his naïve views of love particularly in the lines "The shepherds' swains shall dance and sing / For thy delight each May morning."

The personification of the animals adds to an Eden-like quality also.

In the "Nymph's Reply" we are witnesses to a much harsher view of love. Through its refusal of all the shepherd's almost childlike ideals of love; it begs the question: Does the nymph have something against the shepherd, or is she really a pessimist? She has a sharper and more realistic and more poignant view of love in that it is not necessarily everlasting, just as Eden disappeared. Through a less romantic view of nature, the nymph shows that nothing lasts forever: "Flowers fade." The Nymph shows that she wishes for youth and love to last before she allows herself to love.

The matching structure makes the differences more pronounced. While both poems have the same goal—to obtain love—the ways of attaining that goal make it impossible for the shepherd and the nymph to love each other.

COMMENT ON SAMPLE ESSAY 2

This essay fails to offer an adequate analysis of the two poems. Although there is some analysis, it is incomplete, unconvincing, and sometimes irrelevant. Evidence from the poems is correct in spots, but may be slight or misconstrued in others. The writing demonstrates a lack of control over the conventions of composition and shows an inadequate development of ideas.

QUESTION 4: ON "ON READING POEMS TO A SENIOR CLASS AT SOUTH HIGH" BY D. C. BERRY

In his poem "On Reading Poems to a Senior Class at South High," D. C. Berry reflects on the challenges of teaching. Carefully read the poem. Then write an essay in which you describe Berry's portrayal of teaching and how the poetic devices he uses contribute to the overall effect.

Before
I opened my mouth
I noticed them sitting there
as orderly as frozen fish
in a package.   5

Slowly water began to fill the room
though I did not notice it
till it reached
my ears

and then I heard the sounds   10
of fish in an aquarium
and I knew that though I had
tried to drown them
with my words
that they had only opened up   15
like gills for them
and let me in.

Together we swam around the room
like thirty tails whacking words
till the bell rang   20
puncturing
a hole in the door
where we all leaked out

They went to another class
I suppose and I home   25
where Queen Elizabeth

my cat met me
and licked my fins
till they were hands again.

SAMPLE ESSAY 1

The narrator in "Reading Poems" teaches seniors in high school; his poem is about the act of reading poems to his class. Initially, the narrator is nervous about reading the poems, but as he continues, the class coalesces into a unified group, going on a profound journey, symbolized in the stanza that says "Together we swam around the room / like thirty tails whacking words / till the bell rang." This teacher has genuinely shared a meaningful moment with his class. The author uses an extended metaphor to convey the emotional journey undertaken by the narrator—or any teacher who risks diving into teaching with his whole soul. But it doesn't happen automatically; in the beginning the narrator describes his class as "frozen fish / in a package." They aren't initially responsive to the poems he reads. He envisions them sitting apathetically through his presentation without any interest at all, not even seeming alive. The narrator's nervousness continues to develop as "water began to fill the room," a threatening, overwhelming image, especially given that he "tried to drown them." This really means that he wanted the poems to throw them off, to have a profound effect on them. He does succeed in changing the atmosphere by reading the poem, as symbolized by the change from air to water. Therefore, his nervousness fades as the students join the teacher in his journey. This union is clearly demonstrated through the metaphor as the students "opened up like gills for [his words] and let [the teacher] in." The symbolism of the gills demonstrates that the students are comfortable now in this changed atmosphere—they get the poem. Finally, the bell rings and the students move on as the teacher returns home. The metaphor ends as the teacher returns to human form, thus signifying the end of his journey with his students.

The structure of the poem also contributes to the sense that the poet/teacher has gone through a meaningful experience with his students. The single word "Before" in line 1, standing alone, personifies the teacher, who stands in front of an apparently apathetic class, feeling quite alone. The short lines of each verse and the many enjambments convey the awkwardness of trying to delve into poems—an intimate experience if it is done well—with "strangers." All of the lines are fairly short, producing a long, narrow poem that is like a column going down, into the soul. One of the longest lines is at the center of the poem, and this, significantly, is where the students and teacher "swim" in the poem together.

They say that teachers teach "themselves." In this poem, the poet reveals his teaching self as a sincere person who is willing to take the "plunge" along with his students. There is a necessary transition back to the real world, which his cat "catalyzes."

COMMENT ON SAMPLE ESSAY 1

This highly successful essay offers a range of interpretations, makes specific textual references, and conveys ideas in clear, precise prose. The analysis of the aquarium metaphor and the visual structure of the poem are innovative and convincing. A stronger essay would include more evidence and demonstrate even more sophisticated use of language.

SAMPLE ESSAY 2

In the poem "On Reading Poems to a Senior Class at South High," not only did the author convey his points through his poem, but also he used various literary techniques to further the reader's understanding of teaching poetry. The author of "Reading Poems" uses a metaphor throughout his poem in which the narrator turns into a fish. At the end of the poem, the reader has a better understanding of how poetic techniques are used, too, because he uses enjambment, symbolism, and metaphors.

The narrator in the poem "Reading Poems" teaches seniors in high school and he knows that seniors sometimes don't care about school anymore. So when he reads the poems, he tries to get them to feel some emotions from the poems. But at first he feels their coldness, which he describes using a metaphor of "frozen fish / in a package." The students are frozen in their seats, not listening to him at all. Their faces don't move. They only start to move and act like people when the bell rings and the students can go home. They "swam around the room" "whacking words" because they have not been taught to love poetry, so they rudely mock the poem, ignoring their teacher's efforts. At the end of the poem, the teacher is sort of a fish, so when he goes home, he returns to being a human again. He realizes that no matter how many poems he reads, the kids will never listen or understand, so he begins to question his own career choice.

COMMENT ON SAMPLE ESSAY 2

This essay misses the mark by misconstruing the meaning of some lines and by speculating on topics not addressed by the poem.

QUESTION 5: ON AN EXCERPT FROM "WHERE ARE YOU GOING, WHERE HAVE YOU BEEN?" BY JOYCE CAROL OATES

The following is from the short story "Where Are You Going, Where Have You Been?" by Joyce Carol Oates. In this excerpt, a teenage girl named Connie encounters a boy who will later coerce her into going for a ride with him. Carefully read the passage. Then write an essay in which you describe how the author uses such devices as diction and imagery to convey Connie's innocence, as well as the allure and potential danger of chance encounters.

Sometimes they did go shopping or to a movie, but sometimes they went across the highway, ducking fast across the busy road, to a drive-in restaurant where older kids hung out. The restaurant was shaped like a big bottle, though squatter than a real bottle, and on its 5
cap was a revolving figure of a grinning boy who held a hamburger aloft. One night in mid-summer they ran across, breathless with daring, and right away someone leaned out a car window and invited them over, but it was just a boy from high school they didn't like. It made 10
them feel good to be able to ignore him. They went up through the maze of parked and cruising cars to the bright-lit, fly-infested restaurant, their faces pleased and expectant as if they were entering a sacred building that loomed out of the night to give them what haven and 15
what blessing they yearned for. They sat at the counter and crossed their legs at the ankles, their thin shoulders rigid with excitement, and listened to the music that made everything so good: the music was always in the background like music at a church service, it was 20
something to depend upon.

A boy named Eddie came in to talk with them. He sat backwards on his stool, turning himself jerkily around in semi-circles and then stopping and turning again, and after a while he asked Connie if she would like 25
something to eat. She said she did and so she tapped her friend's arm on her way out—her friend pulled her face up into a brave droll look—and Connie said she would meet her at eleven, across the way. "I just hate to leave her like that," Connie said earnestly, but the boy said 30
that she wouldn't be alone for long. So they went out to his car and on the way Connie couldn't help but let her eyes wander over the windshields and faces all around her, her face gleaming with a joy that had nothing to do with Eddie or even this place; it might have been the 35
music. She drew her shoulders up and sucked in her breath with the pure pleasure of being alive, and just at that moment she happened to glance at a face just a few feet from hers. It was a boy with shaggy black hair, in a convertible jalopy painted gold. He stared at her and 40
then his lips widened into a grin. Connie slit her eyes at

him and turned away, but she couldn't help glancing
back and there he was still watching her. He wagged a
finger and laughed and said, "Gonna get you, baby," and
Connie turned away again without Eddie noticing   45
anything.

She spent three hours with him, at the restaurant
where they ate hamburgers and drank Cokes in wax
cups that were always sweating, and then down an alley
a mile or so away, and when he left her off at five to   50
eleven only the movie house was still open at the plaza.
Her girl friend was there, talking with a boy. When
Connie came up the two girls smiled at each other and
Connie said, "How was the movie?" and the girl said,
"*You* should know." They rode off with the girl's father,   55
sleepy and pleased, and Connie couldn't help but look at
the darkened shopping plaza with its big empty parking
lot and its signs that were faded and ghostly now, and
over at the drive-in restaurant where cars were still
circling tirelessly. She couldn't hear the music at this   60
distance.

Next morning June asked her how the movie was
and Connie said, "So-so."

SAMPLE ESSAY 1

The innocent, those who are yet untouched by the harshness of the
world, seem invariably drawn to those aspects of life that will corrupt
them. They subconsciously seek to be tainted, to do away with the
fragile parts of themselves and become "adults"—or at least, what they
imagine adults to be. Such is the mindset of Connie in Joyce Carol
Oates's short story "Where Are You Going, Where Have You Been?" She
exists in a world where every image she encounters seems to symbolize
her closed and sheltered life: The "revolving figure of a grinning boy who
held a hamburger aloft" that adorns the restaurant that Connie and her
date attend represents the epitome of simpler, more innocent times. It
calls to memory quaint scenes of eating at a café in the 1950s, a time
when much of America was shutting itself off from anything it did not
wish to think about, whether the unfamiliar ways of foreigners or the
dark secrets that dwelled outside of suburbia. Oates's story, written in
the mid-1960s, harkens back to an era in which this mindset was in a
state of upheaval. Philosophies from Eastern countries began to find
their ways across the Atlantic, while the young "hippie" movement
advocated nontraditionalism and cultural revolution. The mere context in
which "Where Are You Going, Where Have You Been?" was written
signifies a state of fading innocence, of ascent into the unknown.

Although Connie is at the age of slowly becoming an adult, Oates
reveals certain immaturities in her and her friends that demonstrate
that she is not yet fully acquainted with the true nature of the world.

Like many high school students, she forms cliques and excludes those she does not deem worthy; she is able to "feel good to be able to ignore [them]," as if the feelings of those being ignored do not amount to anything. Once Connie experiences enough of life, she, too, will feel more empathy. As of now, however, Connie is immature, but the story indicates that this immaturity will be stripped from her by force.

For Connie, like many teenagers, not only fails to resist the dark parts of life, she actively pursues them. Although a complacent and comfortable life may be easy, deep down inside every human being there is a hunger for excitement, for danger, even if it means the loss of our innocence. When Connie first encounters the man who will later abduct her, and who makes his shadiness abundantly clear with his unnerving declaration, "Gonna get you, baby," she cannot help but be enticed by this figure. Unlike boys such as Eddie, who are so bland that Oates feels no need to directly quote anything they say, this person is mysterious and attractive, with his "shaggy black hair" and his otherworldly "convertible jalopy painted gold." Connie knows that this boy will be trouble for her, and though she abruptly looks away from him, he nonetheless stands out to her, as a figure of significance. He cannot be ignored; such is his powerful, dark, and foreboding nature. And it is that exact nature that draws Connie in, even though she knows that it will mean the erasure of her comfortable innocence.

COMMENT ON SAMPLE ESSAY 1
The historical information skirts dangerously close to going off-topic, and although the writer does not indulge too long in it and manages quite deftly to connect it to the thesis, she does so at the expense of textual evidence that would strengthen the argument. However, this essay's sophisticated language, apt quoted evidence, and incisive analysis put it in the upper range.

SAMPLE ESSAY 2

Connie's body language, when she encounters the boy with shaggy black hair, portrays her as innocent yet attracted to possibly dangerous chance encounters. Joyce Carol Oates's diction makes Connie's presence at the bottle shaped restaurant uncomfortable, as if she didn't belong. Oates uses imagery to depict the restaurant as a place of danger for Connie, it is the place where older kids hang out and it makes Connie breathless with daring. Connie has thin shoulders and she crosses her legs at her ankles like a young girl. The one boy she knows likes to spin on the stool and acts impatient and childish. The danger in the situation is clear; the guy who scares her has "black" hair and drives a convertible—*bad guy.* His language makes him seem like someone ready to prey on his next target. The image of him wagging his finger, choosing Connie to be his victim, stands out because of how clear his aggression is. Connie doesn't tell Eddie about what happened; she would rather be with that *bad* kid.

The language in the first paragraph doesn't even question Connie's age, it is about her maturity. Connie is weak; music is the only connection that she has to this group of people whom she envies. In the second paragraph she encounters a bad looking kid, but keeps her experience to herself. The way she slits her eyes hides something, perhaps a liking of the boy with the shaggy black hair—a desire to ride in his convertible. The connection she has with him is something very different. She spends the evening with Eddie but wants to spend her time with the other boy. Her movie was "So-so" because she had to spend it with the nice boy who liked to spin around in his chair like a child. She is the one who will violate her own determination in the end.

COMMENT ON SAMPLE ESSAY 2

While this essay includes some thoughtful interpretation, it lacks proper organization and is not fully developed. Facts from the passage are presented as evidence, but the claims are not fully supported with analysis.

QUESTION 6: ON AN EXCERPT FROM "A&P" BY JOHN UPDIKE

Read the following excerpt from John Updike's 1960 short story "A&P." The passage comes at the end of the story, after the nineteen-year-old protagonist has impetuously quit his job as cash register clerk in an A&P grocery store because the store manager, Lengel, upbraided three teenage girls for coming into the store wearing nothing but bathing suits. Write an essay that describes how humor contributes to the meaning of the passage as a whole.

The girls, and who'd blame them, are in a hurry to get out, so I say "I quit" to Lengel quick enough for them to hear, hoping they'll stop and watch me, their unsuspected hero. They keep right on going, into the electric eye; the door flies open and they flicker across   5 the lot to their car, Queenie and Plaid and Big Tall Goony-Goony (not that as raw material she was so bad), leaving me with Lengel and a kink in his eyebrow.
"Did you say something, Sammy?"
"I said I quit."   10
"I thought you did."
"You didn't have to embarrass them."
"It was they who were embarrassing us."
I started to say something that came out "Fiddle-de-doo." It's a saying of my grandmother's, and I know she   15 would have been pleased.
"I don't think you know what you're saying," Lengel said.
"I know you don't," I said. "But I do." I pull the bow at the back of my apron and start shrugging it off my   20 shoulders. A couple customers that had been heading for my slot begin to knock against each other, like scared pigs in a chute.
Lengel sighs and begins to look very patient and old and gray. He's been a friend of my parents for years.   25 "Sammy, you don't want to do this to your Mom and Dad," he tells me. It's true, I don't. But it seems to me that once you begin a gesture it's fatal not to go through with it. I fold the apron, "Sammy" stitched in red on the pocket, and put it on the counter, and drop the bow tie   30 on top of it. The bow tie is theirs, if you've ever wondered. "You'll feel this for the rest of your life," Lengel says, and I know that's true, too, but remembering how he made that pretty girl blush makes me so scrunchy inside I punch the No Sale tab and the   35 machine whirs "pee-pul" and the drawer splats out. One advantage to this scene taking place in summer, I can follow this up with a clean exit, there's no fumbling around getting your coat and galoshes, I just saunter into the electric eye in my white shirt that my mother   40 ironed the night before, and the door heaves itself open, and outside the sunshine is skating around the asphalt.

I look around for my girls, but they're gone, of course. There wasn't anybody but some young married screaming with her children about some candy theydidn't get by the door of a powder-blue Falcon station wagon. Looking back in the big windows, over the bags of peat moss and aluminum lawn furniture stacked on the pavement, I could see Lengel in my place in the slot, checking the sheep through. His face was dark gray and his back stiff, as if he'd just had an injection of iron, and my stomach kind of fell as I felt how hard the world was going to be to me hereafter.

45

50

SAMPLE ESSAY 1

Humor helps the reader see the situation from the protagonist's point of view. This excerpt illustrates an ironically comical situation, in a mundane setting. Quitting a job is usually no laughing matter; this teenager especially might have limited his future by quitting this occupation. The use of humor helps display the irony in the idea that although quitting a job is serious and life-altering, the naïve nineteen-year-old's reason for quitting is both humorous and sweetly heroic. The juxtaposition of humor next to seriousness symbolizes a transition from childhood to adulthood in the protagonist.

One of the sources of humor Updike uses is names and nicknames. The narrator calls the adult shoppers animal names, such as "pigs" and "sheep." He does this as a way of asserting a little power over them, something a teenager desperately wants, especially when working in a low-level clerk job. The absurd image created when the protagonist relates customers to "scared pigs in a chute" contributes to the reader's understanding of his world. Caught between a child and an adult, the protagonist is still guided by impulsive decisions; at the same time, he understands the consequences of these choices. Seeing the people waiting in line and comparing them to scared pigs signifies the protagonist's skewed outlook. He also assigns funny, somewhat demeaning nicknames, "Queenie and Plaid and Big Tall Goony-Goony," to the girls in the bathing suits. By doing this, Updike not only illustrates the juvenility of the girls, but also of the protagonist himself. If Updike had chosen to leave this detail out, the reader would not get a sense of the protagonist's immaturity.

There is also humor in the situation. The reader cannot help but laugh at the protagonist when he says, "'I quit' to Lengel quick enough for [the girls] to hear, hoping they'll stop and watch me, their unsuspected hero." This moment of high drama placed in a grocery store underscores the irony in the idea that the protagonist quits his job on a whim in an attempt to impress girls. He makes a step toward adulthood when he realizes his actions will have a drastic effect on his life.

Again, the narrator makes light of a serious situation when he remarks after he leaves, "I could see Lengel in my place in the slot, checking the sheep through." Updike chooses to juxtapose this silly image with the following observation: "His face was dark gray and his back stiff, as if he'd just had an injection of iron, and my stomach kind of fell as I felt how hard the world was going to be to me hereafter." The use of language such as "dark gray," "stiff," and "iron" symbolizes the extreme gravity of the protagonist's sudden decision, the maturity of the store manager, and the lack of maturity in the protagonist. This placement of humor against seriousness represents the protagonist's shift in life, a transformation from boy to man. Updike uses humor to expose contradictions throughout the story, such as those between the protagonist and Lengel, and between maturity and immaturity.

COMMENT ON SAMPLE ESSAY 1

This exceptionally strong essay demonstrates a mature reading and fully develops its analysis of two different humor techniques. It also demonstrates excellent control over—and sheer joy in—writing.

SAMPLE ESSAY 2

Updike uses humor in "A&P" to lighten the mood in a story about a boy who quits his job over some girls. Humor is used to make light of a serious decision, to mock adults as compared to teenagers, and to emphasize Sammy's point of view.

At first, Sammy is happy in his job, until three girls come in wearing bathing suits (which is against the rules) and he realizes he doesn't want to be there anymore. Who wouldn't rather be at the beach? "Queeny and Plaid and Big Tall Goony-Goony" are having more fun than he is. Of course, he has to give them nicknames because he doesn't know them personally, though he wishes he did!

The humor also underscores Sammy's immaturity. He doesn't think before he blurts out, "I quit." This is humorous because he should have thought about the consequences longer, but it is also a serious problem in his life. His parents have known Lengel "for years" and will certainly be disappointed by this sudden decision to try to look good in the eyes of three girls he hasn't even met. When he quits, he says it loud enough for the girls to hear "their unsuspected hero," but they keep walking out the door. Maybe this will teach Sammy that a job is more important than showing off to strangers.

COMMENT ON SAMPLE ESSAY 2

This brief essay has no clear focus and contains insufficient and irrelevant analysis.

QUESTION 7: ON AN EXCERPT FROM *A DOLL HOUSE* BY HENRIK IBSEN

Carefully read the following passage from *A Doll House*, by Henrik Ibsen. Then write an essay showing how the author uses literary techniques to characterize Nora and the nature of her conflict, as well as to provide social commentary.

> NORA: Yes, it's true now, Torvald. When I lived at home with Papa, he told me all his opinions, so I had the same ones too; or if they were different I hid them, since he wouldn't have cared for that. He used to call me his doll-child, and he played with me the way I played with my dolls. Then I came into your house—.   5
>
> . . .
>
> I mean, then I went from Papa's hands into yours. You arranged everything to your own taste, and so I got the same tastes as you—or I pretended to; I can't   10 remember. I guess a little of both, first one, then the other. Now when I look back, it seems as if I'd lived here like a beggar—just from hand to mouth. I've lived by doing tricks for you, Torvald. But that's the way you wanted it. It's a great sin what you and Papa   15 did to me. You're to blame that nothing's become of me. . . .
>
> [Y]ou neither think nor talk like the man I could join myself to. When your big fright was over—and it wasn't from any threat against me, only for what   20 might damage you—when all the danger was past, for you it was just as if nothing had happened. I was exactly the same, your little lark, your doll, that you'd have to handle with double care now that I'd turned out so brittle and frail. Torvald—in that instant it   25 dawned on me that for eight years I've been living here with a stranger, and that I'd even conceived three children—oh, I can't stand the thought of it! I could tear myself to bits!

SAMPLE ESSAY 1

In the long monologue from "A Doll House" by Henrik Ibsen, the speaker, Nora, believes that she has been treated as the "doll." I believe that she thinks of herself as a "doll" in a negative way in contrast to what most people consider the endearing characteristics of a doll such as beauty and perfection. However, Nora tragically admits that her doll-like characteristics include mindlessness and emotional absence. Nora knows that she has been treated like a doll or puppet for her entire life by the men who sought to control her. To Nora, these men have literally filled her heart with their own opinions, likes, and dislikes, without ever allowing her to form her own views of her life and the world.

I think that Ibsen takes a very interesting approach to revealing Nora's dilemma; the approach that he uses evokes a response of empathy as well as sympathy in the audience for Nora. Ibsen portrays Nora as the consummate victim, someone who has been lead into thinking of her life as one that is filled with affluence and love, but then finding out that the exact opposite is true.

The ending of this monologue shows that she is horrified by what these men in her life have said and done to her. When she married, life was not a new experience, but rather a transfer from one manager to another, from father to husband. When Nora realizes she has been transferred it uncovers deep feelings and passions she has never known. She objects to the fact that men have been making decisions for her. She is angry with these men, one her husband with whom she had "even conceived three children," and the other her father to whom she was merely "his doll-child," for whom she "lived by doing tricks," and how, "he played with me the way I played with my dolls." To top it off, she is also angry with herself for never realizing that her love was so "brittle and frail," and that she has lived her life for others, and not for herself. She says with a painful self-realization, "I could tear myself to bits."

Of the many poetic devices that Ibsen sprinkles through the prose that he uses, two such devices clearly stand out—these devices are metaphor and simile. They each amplify responses of the audience to her words. In the second paragraph, Nora compares herself to "a beggar— just from hand to mouth." She wants the audience to take pity on her for the cruelty that she has endured from men. Nora is confused and needs to find answers that she may not like, but she is resolute. She knows she must change. But this change may be painful. She must be willing to move away from the childhood security of everything symbolized by the title of the play to the uncertainty of the real adulthood she has yet to experience.

Nora has finally come to the realization that she herself has played a part in the way she has allowed herself to be treated. She says, "nothing's become of me." Nora is faced with a new wave of self-knowledge, and she now wants understanding and respect. I believe that she only now at the end realizes that it might be better to experience an uncertain awareness of self than to be treated as a less-than-equal human. She hopes that this new awareness will be gained by a new triumph. She now sees that a life of being loved by others may simply be glorious deceit. She wants to be free to make mistakes, as well as to succeed.

COMMENT ON SAMPLE ESSAY 1

This essay offers an effective discussion and sensitive exploration of Nora's world before and after her realization. Although there is a tendency to rely too much on plot analysis, the essay shows a sound reading and demonstrates consistent and effective control over the writing. More textual references are needed, but those that are included are apt and specific.

SAMPLE ESSAY 2

Nora appears as a woman who desires independence but may feel that she is not able to be. This passage can be related to a coming of age passage but instead of growing up Nora is learning her true place and the true price she has paid for it since she was a young girl.

Nora desires a mind and a world of her own, but perceives herself as a puppet. The puppeteer being her father and Torvald. Nora holds certain contempt for Torvald saying that he never ever feared about what she would look like or what she even felt like. He was more concerned with how he looked to everyone and how she complimented him.

Her words about her husband and his image can be taken in one of two ways to the reader. One way is that some may think that his concerns were actually valid and that his presentation is key. Also it is important that the reader would know the background of the story and historical context. The time period of this play is very important to understanding it. We cannot judge it by modern standards. Today the standards and outlook of a woman's place in society have drastically changed since the time of the play.

The second way shows a view that the reader may see as one showing Nora as oppressed. She has been kept down for too long as she is ready to burst. Her comments about her dad and her husband show that her thoughts and desires for independence were shunned for far too long. She can no longer be a controlled puppet for this one day at least she bursts, shedding light on her true self and her true thoughts.

COMMENT ON SAMPLE ESSAY 2

Even though the main idea of the passage seems to be present, this less-than-adequate essay shows a mere surface reading of the text. There is awkward phrasing and evidence of misreading. The analysis, too, is off the mark in places and needs to go deeper in others. The clarity of the writing leaves much to be desired. The explanation of the ideas must go deeper and do more in all areas.

QUESTION 8: ON "ACCIDENT" BY DAVE EGGERS

Carefully read Dave Eggers's short-short story "Accident." Then write an essay that describes how the writer uses literary devices such as narrative point of view, selection of detail, syntax, and tone to evoke the narrator's changing perspective on the accident.

You all get out of your cars. You are alone in yours, and there are three teenagers in theirs, an older Camaro in new condition. The accident was your fault, and you walk over to tell them this. Walking over to their car, which you have ruined, it occurs to you that if the three [5] teenagers are angry teenagers, this encounter could be very unpleasant. You pulled into an intersection, obstructing them, and their car hit yours. They have every right to be upset, or livid, or even violence-contemplating. [10]

As you approach, you see that their driver's side door won't open. The driver pushes against it, and you are reminded of scenes where drivers are stuck in submerged cars. Soon they all exit through the passenger side door and walk around the Camaro, inspecting the [15] damage. None of them is hurt, but the car is wrecked. "Just bought this today," the driver says. He is 18, blond, average in all ways. "Today?" you ask.

You are a bad person, you think. You also think: what a dorky car for a teenager to buy in 2005. "Yeah, today," he [20] says, then sighs. You tell him that you are sorry. That you are so, so sorry. That it was your fault and that you will cover all costs.

You exchange insurance information, and you find yourself, minute by minute, ever more thankful that none [25] of these teenagers has punched you, or even made a remark about your being drunk, which you are not, or being stupid, which you are, often. You become more friendly with all of them, and you realize that you are much more connected to them, particularly to the driver, [30] than possible in perhaps any other way.

You have done him and his friends harm, in a way, and you jeopardized their health, and now you are so close you feel like you share a heart. He knows your name and you know his, and you almost killed him and, because [35] you got so close to doing so but didn't, you want to fall on him, weeping, because you are so lonely, so lonely always, and all contact is contact, and all contact makes us so grateful we want to cry and dance and cry and cry.

In a moment of clarity, you finally understand why [40] boxers, who want so badly to hurt each other, can rest their heads on the shoulders of their opponents, can lean against one another like tired lovers, so thankful for a moment of peace.

Sample Essay 1

The first hint that lets the reader know that the point of view is central to understanding this short-short story is the second-person narrator, who addresses himself, oddly, as "you." Now, in everyday conversations, when people address themselves as "you," they do it either to separate themselves from their actions or, the obverse, as a plea for empathy. And in the case of "The Accident," both reasons pertain. The narrator who regrets having just caused a car accident is a lonely person who processes the frightening event as though he has come into intimate contact with the people in the other car, and sadly, for him, it does constitute a moment of intimacy.

At first the narrator is wary, for he knows that the teenagers in the other car "have every right to be upset, or livid, or even violence-contemplating" because the accident is his fault. He is on edge, and is strongly aware of the "us-them" mentality that happens in car accidents. Things could get ugly, he knows. So he immediately takes responsibility, a mature thing and also an honest thing to do, and this apparently diffuses any anger the teenagers might feel. Of course, a teenager who has just bought a new Camaro, a sports car, that very day, has every justification to be angry, so the narrator feels lucky that he isn't violent.

After the required sharing of insurance information, they are all on a first-name basis, apparently, and the tension releases a bit, so the narrator can now let into his consciousness the fact that it is not so important that a new car was damaged, but that lives were put at risk. He has been very lucky indeed not to have harmed another human being, let alone a young person in his or her prime. The relief at not having done so makes the narrator want to "fall" on the driver "weeping," but now we learn that the narrator is lonely, "so lonely, so lonely always." The repetition of the words "lonely," "contact," "grateful," and "cry" not only attests to the narrator's fragile state of mind, but also, through the syntax of the sentence, gives the reader a sense of the boredom and repetition of his days. The sole word "dance" refers to his sheer joy at having contact with other humans, in addition to his relief at not having killed them in the process.

The final paragraph pulls together the narrator's initial edginess and wariness and his desire for intimacy, when he relates the accident to the way that boxers want to hurt each other. The tone of the piece from the beginning indicates how easily one allows unexpected contact with strangers to result in blows, physical or emotional. Yet that deep-seated urge for intimacy is really the reason for it.

Comment on Sample Essay 1

Though it ends abruptly, this essay succeeds in amplifying the meaning of the succinct story. The penultimate paragraph is most impressive because of its sophisticated insights and the maturity of the writing, making a most convincing argument. Overall, the writing is confident and well structured.

Sample Essay 2

In this essay, the author is worried that a teenager whose car he has just hit will beat him up or be angry. So therefore he tries to avoid feeling like a "bad person" and he tells the other driver that it's his fault. He knows that it is his fault, so taking responsibility is the right thing to do. He tells the person he will pay for the damage, which is a lot since the car is "totaled." This is the beginning of a very bad day for him, but at least the teenage driver is not angry with him. With relief, he hangs his head on the shoulder of the other driver, an 18-year-old blond boy, and just cries. Since he is a lonely person, the narrator actually hopes that the other driver will become a friend. Yet overall, he is just thankful that no one punched him, so he can get in his car and drive away. His insurance will cover the expenses. All in all, no harm was done, so his attitude when he leaves the accident is better than it was before the accident.

Comment on Sample Essay 2
This writer not only misrepresents the facts in the story, but also misunderstands the prompt, and therefore fails to analyze the obvious and underlying themes and characterizations. The essay's brevity also lessens its effectiveness.

QUESTION 9: ON SETTING AS CHARACTER

Settings in many great works of literature function like a character. Choose a novel or play with such a setting, and in a well-organized essay, show how the setting contributes to the meaning of the novel or play. You may select either one of the works listed below or another work of comparable literary merit.

A Doll House
A Passage to India
A Raisin in the Sun
Death of a Salesman
Equus
God's Favorite
Great Expectations
Hamlet
Love Medicine
M. Butterfly
Macbeth
Medea
Member of the Wedding
Othello
Our Town

Pride and Prejudice
Pygmalion
Saint Joan
Song of Solomon
The Awakening
The Color Purple
The Great Gatsby
The Joy Luck Club
The Kite Runner
The Merchant of Venice
The Scarlet Letter
The Tempest
The Winter's Tale
Things Fall Apart
Who's Afraid of Virginia Woolf?

SAMPLE ESSAY 1

The most interesting characters in literature are complex, unpredictable, and ambiguous. They are like a few of the people that we meet in life. But not everyone that we meet dazzles us with his or her personality. The fictional town, Grover's Corners, is at least metaphorically no exception. It is no dazzler of a character. It is a gray, beat-up backdrop, an empty canvas, on which we see come to life the play's characters, the inhabitants of *Our Town*.

Wilder makes the character of the town be a drab and ordinary setting for the action of his play. Costume tells a lot about a character; the stage's bleak appearance reveals much about the town. This town barely makes the equally dull lives of its residents stand out until an after-death experience illuminates through just one wonderful day all that was average.

In the beginning of the play, the character of the town makes up the children's entire outer world. The children are secure within the town's borders. The children ask nothing of the town. Their parents, teachers, and friends protect them and meet their needs. The town is unresponsive and un-giving.

The play's other characters also take the town for granted as the children grow up. The advantages of small-town life are overlooked. The residents assume the character of the town will always be there. Most town residents cannot realize day to day how much their lives are changing. They will not appreciate the stability and constancy of the town until they experience chaos.

Other residents have a different point of view and blame the character of the town for holding them back. The smallness of the town excuses their failure to take on adult responsibility. The idea of growing up is idealized and romanticized by the town's adults. It's so nice to grow up. Ironically, the children themselves express realistic fears about growing up. The town's grown-ups are not ready to deal with these fears, and the children have to find their own way. The adult characters and the town are equally unable to help.

The town as a character has other flaws. The audience sees these flaws as it does those of other dramatic characters. The town cruelly betrays others by leading them into a false sense of security, a complacency that they rely on. This reminds me of what it was like at summer camp last year—we never missed the water until the camp's well ran dry.

As in real life, the flaws we see in others and in the town may simply be a reflection of our own flaws. We want other people to depend on us until it is time to be responsible and help them.

The town remains physically the same throughout all three acts of the play, as the years go by in the lives of the residents. Its residents grow up, marry, bear children, and die. The town undergoes no spring clean-up or renovation. The town is always just a silent witness to the lives of the other characters. Eventually, though, the play forces the audience to take a closer look at life in a small town, and perhaps at their own lives.

COMMENT ON SAMPLE ESSAY 1

This essay is a focused and persuasive analysis. It is not without minor flaws, but it generally makes a strong case with significant insight and understanding. It does provide a reasonable analysis of the concept of setting as character and shows the setting's relationship to past events, actions, values, and attitudes. The essay explores relationships and demonstrates how those relationships contribute to the meaning of the work.

SAMPLE ESSAY 2

William Shakespeare's play "The Tragedy of Hamlet" takes place in the kingdom of Denmark. Denmark besides being the setting of the play is in a state of political turmoil after the death of the king, which is later determined to be the result of murder. While defending itself against military invasions from Norway, Denmark's throne is taken over by Claudius, who is the brother of the late king.

In "Hamlet," the setting can be seen as a character, a foil to Hamlet's character revealed throughout the play. The setting can be compared to the character of young Hamlet similarly to the way Fortinbras and later Laertes can be seen as foils to his character. Hamlet hesitates as he contemplates revenge and Denmark as a country also is left with political uncertainty as a result of the same murder.

While Hamlet, Jr., lost his father, Denmark lost its king. In the play the setting can be seen as a somewhat static character. Although it is crucial to the series of events that unfold throughout the plot, the setting is flat in the way it acts as a foil to Hamlet's character. The turmoil in Denmark represents the turmoil in Hamlet. This uncertainty also applies to Denmark and its future leaders.

If Hamlet killed Claudius and survives would he have become king? Why did Claudius assume the throne after old Hamlet's death? Who is to blame for the downfall of the main characters in the play's tragic ending? Denmark's unknown future as a kingdom adds to the uncertainty as a theme.

Although not an entirely dynamic character that takes a direct role in the action, Denmark undergoes several changes as the plot twists and develops, just as Hamlet experienced many changes in his life up until his tragic end.

COMMENT ON SAMPLE ESSAY 2

This essay has elements of the superficial and the obvious. It uses some vague details from the text, which are correct. The commentary tends to be generic, but there is some analysis and some understanding of what is being asked. The essay is much too short and deals with the political situation in Denmark instead of the actual setting. The conclusion of the essay is inadequate. It depends on plot, enumeration of deaths and political situations and drifts away from an analysis and commentary on the physical setting as character. To compound those errors, the writing is poor.

QUESTION 10: ON COMEDY

Aristotle suggested that comedy shows average or below-average people who enjoy a transition from bad circumstances to good. The critic Northrop Frye believed that in comedy, "the device that brings hero and heroine together causes a new society to crystallize around the hero."

From a novel or play, choose an average or below-average humorous character. Then write a well-organized essay in which you identify how and why that character makes us laugh as he or she moves from good to bad circumstances and helps to bring about a new society. Explain how the author's treatment of the character contributes to the meaning of the work as a whole. You may choose one from the list below or another play or novel of similar literary merit.

A Midsummer Night's Dream
Androcles and the Lion
Barefoot In The Park
Breakfast of Champions
Candide
Catch-22
Cyrano de Bergerac
Don Quixote
Endgame
Harvey
Juno and the Paycock
Lady Windermere's Fan
Lysistrata
Member of the Wedding
One Flew Over the Cuckoo's Nest

Penguin Island
Rosencrantz and Guildenstern
   Are Dead
Pygmalion
She Stoops to Conquer
Tartuffe
The Bald Soprano
The Brute
The Importance of Being Earnest
The Odd Couple
The Rivals
The Sandbox
The Tempest
Tom Jones
Waiting for Godot

SAMPLE ESSAY 1

Comedy as a genre is elusive and difficult to explain to everyone's satisfaction. The comic nature of a work of literature is almost never a constant because everyone laughs at different things. Tragedy, on the other hand, is obvious. Comedy and comic characters are often dismissed by literary elitists. Although the essential quality of comedy centers on some form of incongruity that seems to be present in all comedy, it is extremely challenging to say exactly why something, or someone, is funny. Aside from this element of incongruity, there are other commonalties. It seems that all humorous people and funny actions possess at least one of the following elements: physical humor, an ability to relate the person or action to human nature, and an openly preposterous action or person.

The physical humor occurs in literature through the use of subtext and context. The comparison of funny actions and funny people to normal people gives a hint of why we laugh. The constant reliance on the ridiculous stands in stark opposition to the norm.

Comedy, like so many elemental things in life and literature, often escapes an easy definition because what is comedy to one observer may be stupidity to another. Comedy does allow us to take a close look at ourselves as human beings through the proxy of comic characters and comic situations.

The comic character Sir John Falstaff appears in William Shakespeare's "Part I of Henry IV, " "Part II of Henry IV," and "The Merry Wives of Windsor." I think that Jack Falstaff as a great comic character, a madcap charlatan, in a great comedy such as "Part I of Henry IV" fulfills all the requirements for an archetype of the lovable bumbling fool. He is portrayed as a consummate drunkard who is rarely, if ever, sober. He is shown to be humorous by all but the most puritanical. His characterization ties social dialogue to our shared understanding of what it means to be human.

Falstaff is free of the constraints of the everyday world that surrounds us; he is detached from any. His context is defined by the lack of any conventional reason and morality. As the comic speaker, he gains from his lack of adherence to anything that is usually considered to be typical behavior. His humor mainly lies in the absurdity of his actions and the cleverness of his speech. He takes much pleasure in playing the role and he is pleased to be the brunt of most jokes by his so-called friends. He is always trying to separate hard-working people from their hard-earned money. His actions are not laudable, but he does what we in our wildest moments dream of doing. He may represent our desires for secret pleasures. He is always trying to make the somber Hal laugh. He always gets away with being less than we are. His lack of a conscience stands in direct contrast to normal action in the real world. No matter what he does, he always seems to come out on top.

We can also relate to Falstaff's words and misuse of logic. We are forced to see a lot of ourselves in Jack Falstaff. The audience laughs at Jack Falstaff because we think about how different our lives and personalities are in contrast to his classic "court jester" persona. He is like the little kid that we once were who constantly told stupid "elephant" jokes. We delight in the utter triteness of his jokes but we have matured and passed that stage in our lives. We still enjoy and cling to the nostalgia of our youth, which is echoed in his puns, such as when he tells Hal (and us) that the bottle of sherry stowed away in his pistol case will "Sack a city."

We are amused at his flights of fancy and constant misuse of logic, especially as he gives us a catechism on the stupidity of the concept "honor." We wonder how anyone could keep a straight face as Falstaff tells the amusing barefaced lies about the Gad's Hill robbery of the robbers. We have grown and matured, but, alas, he has not.

Falstaff's actions force us to think about why inebriated people seem to be funny to most observers. We are forced to ask ourselves, "Why do we laugh at drunks?" and "What is there about Falstaff's way of life that is so alluring?" In a very strange way we can all relate to him. Falstaff acts as a foil and holds a mirror up to human nature for us. It is, however, a distorted funhouse image that we see. We need this distorted image to laugh at our imperfections and ourselves.

COMMENT ON SAMPLE ESSAY 1

This essay has the qualities that make for a superior paper. The prompt to the question is very difficult, and the student has presented a convincing response. The essay depends heavily on plot summary, but the analysis is worthwhile. Overall, the essay demonstrates the writer's ability to discuss a literary work with insight and control. There are times it is well-written, but often it shows a lack of control and sophistication. However, it stays focused and offers an opinion about meaning.

SAMPLE ESSAY 2

Horace Walpole says that the world is a comedy to those who think, and a tragedy to those who feel. So I ask myself: Which is better? Thinking or feeling? Well I for one would rather laugh than cry.

To me the idea of average people doing average things or better yet average people doing below-average things is appealing and entertaining. It is not entertaining because we "feel" how the person must feel, or relate and feel the consequences of an action. Comedy to me is entertaining because I think about when I too have acted silly just like a character in a story. And when I hear comedy I am able to let go of any bad feelings that I have as I am forced to think of good ones.

In the novel "One Flew Over the Cuckoo's Nest" we read about a bunch of crazy people constantly fooling around. If we really feel empathy for this situation it may be very hurtful, but if we let go of our controls and think about it for a while, it becomes hilarious. The characters in the novel move from bad to good when they give up on everything that people told them that they could not do. They did all of this by remaining true to themselves. What made the novel funny for me was the main character's insanity, which doesn't change throughout the story. The novel's approach to comedy enables the reader to dispute all reality as it tears at the very fiber of reality. It shows us something that is far more real.

McMurphy is the main comic character who stands for individuality and free expression. One idea presented is that one man's freedom can be equated with the government. He battles against letting the oppressive society he finds himself in turn him into a machine. He keeps his individuality until the end, but is eventually destroyed. He is filled with unwarranted passions, and willful self-deception.

The only thing that really changes is how people treat McMurphy when they believe in him. Now that makes us think. When a society thinks, then society throws back its collective head and laughs. To me the best comedy in the novel came as the main character wins as he loses. He assumes that he can fool everyone. Then the comedy really works. He not only fools others, but he eventually fools himself and in so doing he even fools the reader. The novel asks two questions: Are all the sane people crazy? Are all the crazy people sane? The answers as presented in the novel are a delight.

The main character is shown by the author to be in direct contrast to all of the other characters, especially to Nurse Ratchet, who is a flat character. She undergoes little or no change throughout the novel. She began as a crafty and manipulative character and remains the same through to the novel's conclusion, while McMurphy is dynamic and constantly changes.

Comedy, therefore, is about getting inside the minds of the readers. When the readers view the comedy and comic characters they are forced to think about how they themselves appear in their daily social events and the whole thing may be very funny, but it teaches the reader an introspective and valuable lesson on life.

COMMENT ON SAMPLE ESSAY 2

This essay shows unrefined thinking about this difficult prompt. It is not well-conceived, -organized, or -developed, and it demonstrates inconsistent control over many of the elements of composition. The writing is insufficient to convey the writer's ideas, and it is often so inaccurate that it does not clearly relate to the prompt or the novel being discussed. It contains too little supporting evidence to prove the student's contentions.

Part III

Complete Practice Tests

PRACTICE TEST 1

AP ENGLISH LITERATURE AND COMPOSITION EXAMINATION
Section I: Multiple-Choice Questions
Number of questions: 55
Total time: 1 hour

Directions: This part consists of selections from prose works and questions on their content, form, and style. After reading each passage, choose the best answer to each question.

QUESTIONS 1–13. Carefully read "Blackberry Eating" by Galway Kinnell before choosing your answers.

I love to go out in late September
among the fat, overripe, icy, black blackberries
to eat blackberries for breakfast,
the stalks very prickly, a penalty
they earn for knowing the black art   5
of blackberry-making; and as I stand among them
lifting the stalks to my mouth, the ripest berries
fall almost unbidden to my tongue,
as words sometimes do, certain peculiar words
like *strengths* or *squinched,*   10
many-lettered, one-syllabled lumps,
which I squeeze, squinch open, and splurge well
in the silent, startled, icy, black language
of blackberry-eating in late September.

1. The meter of the poem is
   (A) trochaic
   (B) alternating tetrameter and trimeter
   (C) free verse
   (D) iambic pentameter
   (E) alexandrine

2. The poetic technique most frequently used in this poem is
   (A) alliteration
   (B) assonance
   (C) consonance
   (D) simile
   (E) internal rhyme

3. The subject of the main clause in the sentence that begins "and as I stand . . ." (line 6) is
   (A) I (line 6)
   (B) stalks (line 7)
   (C) berries (line 7)
   (D) tongue (line 8)
   (E) words (line 9)

4. The subject of the poem is primarily
   (A) the ripeness of September
   (B) the influence of language
   (C) the quiet joy of solitude
   (D) "the black art"
   (E) the sensuous sounds of words

5. "[T]he black art" (line 5) connotes
   (A) African-American art
   (B) magic
   (C) photosynthesis
   (D) reproduction
   (E) life

6. "[U]nbidden" (line 8) means
   (A) unrequited
   (B) uninvited
   (C) unwarranted
   (D) unwanted
   (E) unbeknownst

7. The poet values certain one-syllable words such as "squinched" (line 10) for their
   (A) distinctiveness
   (B) concision
   (C) arcaneness
   (D) mellifluousness
   (E) lusciousness

8. The tone of the poem is
   (A) hyperbolic
   (B) ceremonial
   (C) sanctimonious
   (D) blissful
   (E) jubilant

9. The form of the poem is a(n)
   (A) English sonnet
   (B) Italian sonnet
   (C) quatorzain
   (D) villanelle
   (E) Spenserian sonnet

10. The poem does all of the following EXCEPT
    (A) alludes to time's decay
    (B) expresses wonder at creation
    (C) celebrates the poet's creativity
    (D) acknowledges the poet's joy in being alive
    (E) compares eating fruit to enjoying language

11. In the context of the poem, the word "icy" in lines 2 and 13 could be replaced with
    (A) sharp
    (B) crystalline
    (C) distinguished
    (D) refreshing
    (E) rare

12. Essentially, the poem is about writing
    (A) in general
    (B) poems
    (C) as a surrogate for life
    (D) as an agreeable pastime
    (E) as the outcome of reflection

13. The poem is primarily
    (A) sensory
    (B) cerebral
    (C) ironic
    (D) symbolic
    (E) philosophical

QUESTIONS 14–26. Carefully read "I Go Back to May 1937" by Sharon Olds before choosing your answers.

I see them standing at the formal gates of their colleges,
I see my father strolling out
under the ochre sandstone arch, the
red tiles glinting like bent
plates of blood behind his head, I   5
see my mother with a few light books at her hip
standing at the pillar made of tiny bricks with the
wrought-iron gate still open behind her, its
sword-tips black in the May air,
they are about to graduate, they are about to get married, 10
they are kids, they are dumb, all they know is they are
innocent, they would never hurt anybody.
I want to go up to them and say Stop,
don't do it—she's the wrong woman,
he's the wrong man, you are going to do things   15
you cannot imagine you would ever do,
you are going to do bad things to children,
you are going to suffer in ways you never heard of,
you are going to want to die. I want to go
up to them there in the late May sunlight and say it,   20
her hungry pretty blank face turning to me,
her pitiful beautiful untouched body,
his arrogant handsome blind face turning to me,
his pitiful beautiful untouched body,
but I don't do it. I want to live. I   25
take them up like the male and female
paper dolls and bang them together
at the hips like chips of flint as if to
strike sparks from them, I say
Do what you are going to do, and I will tell about it.   30

14. The poem includes all of the following EXCEPT
    (A) apostrophe
    (B) anaphora
    (C) imagery
    (D) hyperbole
    (E) parallelism

15. There are shifts in mood at lines
    (A) 5 and 10
    (B) 13 and 19
    (C) 13 and 25
    (D) 14 and 17
    (E) 19 and 29

16. The tone of the poem, overall, is
    (A) nostalgic
    (B) impish
    (C) imperious
    (D) acerbic
    (E) baleful

17. The word "ochre" (line 3) means
    (A) yellowish orange
    (B) archaic
    (C) imposing
    (D) gothic
    (E) arched

18. The diction of the poem is primarily
    (A) Latinate
    (B) colloquial
    (C) formal
    (D) erudite
    (E) Anglo-Saxon

19. The imagery in lines 1–9
    (A) connotes the passage of time
    (B) presages danger
    (C) symbolizes death
    (D) evokes a rite of passage
    (E) underscores a sense of formality

20. The imagery in lines 25–30 reinforces a theme of
    (A) artificiality
    (B) intransigence
    (C) discord
    (D) courtship
    (E) spring

21. Which of the following images hint at trouble to come?
    I. "bent / plates of blood" (lines 4–5)
    II. "wrought-iron gate still open behind her" (line 8)
    III. "sword-tips black in the May air" (line 9)
    (A) I and II only
    (B) I only
    (C) II and III only
    (D) I, II, and III
    (E) I and III only

22. The poem moves from
    (A) reverie, to recollection, to resignation
    (B) reminiscence, to realism, to prophecy
    (C) curiosity, to anger, to love
    (D) fantasy, to history, to future
    (E) unreality, to certainty, to authenticity

23. Lines 2–5 illustrate
    (A) satire
    (B) ambiguity
    (C) personification
    (D) enjambment
    (E) allusion

24. "I Go Back to May 1937" is an example of a(n)
    (A) epithalamium
    (B) elegy
    (C) sonnet
    (D) narrative poem
    (E) lyric poem

25. The image of "sparks" flying from "chips of flint" (lines 28–29)
    represents
    (A) the crucible of her parents' love
    (B) both antagonism and attraction in the parents' relationship
    (C) that her parents are essentially the same
    (D) the depth of her parents' hatred for each other
    (E) the narrator's misunderstanding of her parents

26. The groups of lines that begin with the same words (17–19; 21–24)
    contribute to a sense of the narrator's
    (A) pain
    (B) envy
    (C) hysteria
    (D) frustration
    (E) dogmatism

QUESTIONS 27–41. Carefully read "Let me not to the marriage of true minds" by William
Shakespeare before choosing your answers.

> Let me not to the marriage of true minds
> Admit impediments. Love is not love
> Which alters when it alteration finds,
> Or bends with the remover to remove:
> Oh, no! it is an ever-fixéd mark,   5
> That looks on tempests and is never shaken;
> It is the star to every wandering bark,
> Whose worth's unknown, although his height be taken.
> Love's not Time's fool, though rosy lips and cheeks
> Within his bending sickle's compass come;   10
> Love alters not with his brief hours and weeks,
> But bears it out even to the edge of doom.
>   If this be error and upon me proved,
>   I never writ, nor no man ever loved.

27. In the context of the first line, "Admit" (line 2) means
    (A) accept
    (B) concede
    (C) let in
    (D) tolerate
    (E) grant

28. The word "impediments" (line 2) means
    (A) hindrances
    (B) flaws
    (C) improprieties
    (D) infidelities
    (E) disharmony

29. The meter of the poem is
    (A) iambic tetrameter
    (B) trochaic tetrameter
    (C) anapestic pentameter
    (D) iambic pentameter
    (E) dactylic trimeter

30. Line 3 includes a(n)
    (A) asyndeton
    (B) polyptoton
    (C) portmanteau word
    (D) appositive
    (E) archetype

31. The poem says that true love is
    (A) steadfast
    (B) rare
    (C) resilient
    (D) conjugal
    (E) generous

32. The antecedent of the pronoun "It" (line 7) is
    (A) marriage (line 1)
    (B) minds (line 1)
    (C) love (line 2)
    (D) alteration (line 3)
    (E) mark (line 5)

33. The word "bark" (line 7) means
    (A) boat
    (B) cleric
    (C) wind
    (D) outcast
    (E) nomad

34. The last two lines comprise a(n)
    (A) internal rhyme
    (B) heroic couplet
    (C) hyperbole
    (D) authorial aside
    (E) paradox

35. Much of the diction in lines 5–8 can be described as
    (A) decorous
    (B) forensic
    (C) statutory
    (D) nautical
    (E) solicitous

36. "Whose worth's unknown, although his height be taken" (line 8)
    refers to
    (A) the narrator
    (B) "an ever-fixéd mark" (line 5)
    (C) "star" (line 7)
    (D) "bark" (line 7)
    (E) the addressee of the poem

37. Line 8 compares
    (A) quality with quantity
    (B) the sublime with the customary
    (C) the surreal with the real
    (D) immeasurability and measurability
    (E) time and eternity

38. The poem includes all of the following EXCEPT
    (A) alliteration
    (B) masculine rhyme
    (C) apostrophe
    (D) personification
    (E) rich rhyme

39. In the context of the poem, to not be "Time's fool" (line 9) would
    imply that love
    (A) bows to time's dominion
    (B) cherishes each moment
    (C) ignores the aging process
    (D) can occur at any time
    (E) lasts for all of eternity

40. In the last two lines, the poet is essentially saying
    (A) Time will tell if I am right
    (B) I cannot be proven wrong
    (C) Only your love can prove me right
    (D) No man has loved as I love you
    (E) I have never written truer words

41. The tone of the poem is
    (A) haughty
    (B) scolding
    (C) authoritarian
    (D) self-assured
    (E) imploring

QUESTIONS 42–55. Carefully read the following passage from the beginning of Gabriel García Márquez's short story "A Very Old Man with Enormous Wings" before choosing your answers.

On the third day of rain they had killed so many crabs inside the house that Pelayo had to cross his drenched courtyard and throw them into the sea, because the newborn child had a temperature all night and they thought it was due to the stench. The world had been sad since Tuesday. Sea and sky were a single ash-gray thing and the sands of the beach, which on March nights glimmered like powdered light, had become a stew of mud and rotten shellfish. The light was so weak at noon that when Pelayo was coming back to the house after throwing away the crabs, it was hard for him to see what it was that was moving and groaning in the rear of the courtyard. He had to go very close to see that it was an old man, a very old man, lying face down in the mud, who, in spite of his tremendous efforts, couldn't get up, impeded by his enormous wings.

Frightened by that nightmare, Pelayo ran to get Elisenda, his wife, who was putting compresses on the sick child, and he took her to the rear of the courtyard. They both looked at the fallen body with mute stupor. He was dressed like a ragpicker. There were only a few faded hairs left on his bald skull and very few teeth in his mouth, and his pitiful condition of a drenched great-grandfather had taken away any sense of grandeur he might have had. His huge buzzard wings, dirty and half-plucked, were forever entangled in the mud. They looked at him so long and so closely that Pelayo and Elisenda very soon overcame their surprise and in the end found him familiar. Then they dared speak to him, and he answered in an incomprehensible dialect with a strong sailor's voice. That was how they skipped over the inconvenience of the wings and quite intelligently concluded that he was a lonely castaway from some foreign ship wrecked by the storm. And yet, they called in a neighbor woman who knew everything about life and death to see him, and all she needed was one look to show them their mistake.

"He's an angel," she told them. "He must have been coming for the child, but the poor fellow is so old that the rain knocked him down."

On the following day everyone knew that a flesh-and-blood angel was held captive in Pelayo's house. Against the judgment of the wise neighbor woman, for whom angels in those times were the fugitive survivors of a celestial conspiracy, they did not have the heart to club him to death. Pelayo watched over him all afternoon from the kitchen, armed with his bailiff's club, and before going to bed he dragged him out of the mud and locked him up with the hens in the wire

5

10

15

20

25

30

35

40

45

chicken coop. In the middle of the night, when the rain
stopped, Pelayo and Elisenda were still killing crabs. A
short time afterward the child woke up without a fever
and with a desire to eat. Then they felt magnanimous
and decided to put the angel on a raft with fresh water
and provisions for three days and leave him to his fate
on the high seas. But when they went out into the
courtyard with the first light of dawn, they found the
whole neighborhood in front of the chicken coop having
fun with the angel, without the slightest reverence,
tossing him things to eat through the openings in the
wire as if he weren't a supernatural creature but a circus
animal.

Father Gonzaga arrived before seven o'clock,
alarmed at the strange news. By that time onlookers less
frivolous than those at dawn had already arrived and
they were making all kinds of conjectures concerning
the captive's future. The simplest among them thought
that he should be named mayor of the world. Others of
sterner mind felt that he should be promoted to the rank
of five-star general in order to win all wars. Some
visionaries hoped that he could be put to stud in order to
implant on earth a race of winged wise men who could
take charge of the universe. But Father Gonzaga, before
becoming a priest, had been a robust woodcutter.
Standing by the wire, he reviewed his catechism in an
instant and asked them to open the door so that he could
take a close look at that pitiful man who looked more like
a huge decrepit hen among the fascinated chickens. He
was lying in a corner drying his open wings in the
sunlight among the fruit peels and breakfast leftovers
that the early risers had thrown him. Alien to the
impertinences of the world, he only lifted his antiquarian
eyes and murmured something in his dialect when
Father Gonzaga went into the chicken coop and said
good morning to him in Latin. The parish priest had his
first suspicion of an imposter when he saw that he did
not understand the language of God or know how to
greet His ministers. Then he noticed that seen close up
he was much too human: he had an unbearable smell of
the outdoors, the back side of his wings was strewn with
parasites and his main feathers had been mistreated by
terrestrial winds, and nothing about him measured up to
the proud dignity of angels. Then he came out of the
chicken coop and in a brief sermon warned the curious
against the risks of being ingenuous. He reminded them
that the devil had the bad habit of making use of carnival
tricks in order to confuse the unwary. He argued that if
wings were not the essential element in determining the
difference between a hawk and an airplane, they were
even less so in the recognition of angels. Nevertheless,
he promised to write a letter to his bishop so that the
latter would write to his primate so that the latter would

write to the Supreme Pontiff in order to get the final
verdict from the highest courts.

His prudence fell on sterile hearts. The news of the   105
captive angel spread with such rapidity that after a few
hours the courtyard had the bustle of a marketplace and
they had to call in troops with fixed bayonets to disperse
the mob that was about to knock the house down.
Elisenda, her spine all twisted from sweeping up so   110
much marketplace trash, then got the idea of fencing in
the yard and charging five cents admission to see the
angel.

42. The point of view of the narrator is
    (A) omniscient
    (B) first-person limited
    (C) third-person limited
    (D) unreliable
    (E) naïve

43. The imagery of the setting described in the first paragraph
    (A) presages a deluge
    (B) heralds an epic
    (C) signifies poverty
    (D) implies contamination
    (E) reveals a magical realm

44. All of the following roles are considered for the old man EXCEPT
    to
    (A) take the sick child to heaven
    (B) take over the world
    (C) reprimand the town sinners
    (D) defend the town
    (E) father a new race

45. In the second paragraph, the old man is described in terms that
    make him seem
    (A) celestial
    (B) pitiable
    (C) deceitful
    (D) puzzled
    (E) execrable

46. The phrase "quite intelligently concluded" (line 32) in the context of
    the sentence is
    (A) mystifying
    (B) understandable
    (C) overly simplistic
    (D) ironic
    (E) characteristic

47. The tone of the passage is
    (A) insinuating
    (B) skeptical
    (C) sardonic
    (D) detached
    (E) bemused

48. Pelayo's act of enclosing the old man in a chicken coop connotes
    (A) economic prowess
    (B) an unhealthy desire to control his environment
    (C) a misinterpretation of God's will
    (D) religious apostasy
    (E) spiritual impoverishment

49. Overall, the story is
    (A) serio-comic
    (B) blasphemous
    (C) juvenile
    (D) allegorical
    (E) sacrosanct

50. The second paragraph includes all of the following EXCEPT
    (A) imagery
    (B) analogy
    (C) hyperbole
    (D) understatement
    (E) an appositive

51. Pelayo's interest in the old man moves from
    (A) curiosity, to fear, to exploitation
    (B) disdain, to apathy, to confusion
    (C) fear, to reverence, to manipulation
    (D) obligation, to adulation, to revulsion
    (E) caution, to respect, to deference

52. At different times, the townspeople see the old man as all of the following EXCEPT a(n)
    (A) trickster
    (B) potential savior
    (C) alien
    (D) castaway sailor
    (E) angel

53. The theme of the excerpt is
    (A) greed
    (B) divine revelation
    (C) the bane of poverty
    (D) human folly
    (E) celestial inscrutability

54. Father Gonzaga's reaction after speaking Latin to the old man reveals his
    (A) reverence
    (B) erudition
    (C) ignorance
    (D) piety
    (E) sense of humor

55. The story exemplifies the statement
    (A) The poor cannot afford piety
    (B) The ignorant are easily tricked
    (C) The Church has lost credibility
    (D) God works in mysterious ways
    (E) Faith is trust without reservation

STOP
END OF SECTION I

Section II: Essay Questions
Number of questions: 3
Reading time: 15 minutes
Writing time: 2 hours

Directions: Section II of this examination requires answers in essay form. The two hours are yours to divide among the three essay questions as you think best. To help you use your time well, the proctor may announce the time at which each question should be completed. If you finish any question before time is announced, you may go on to another question. You may go back at any time and work on any essay question you want.

Each essay will be judged on its clarity and effectiveness in dealing with the assigned topic and on the quality of the writing. In response to Question 3, select a work of recognized literary merit appropriate to the question. A good general rule is to use works of the same quality as those you studied in your Advanced Placement literature course(s).

After completing each question, you should check your essay for accuracy of punctuation, spelling, and diction; you are advised, however, not to attempt many longer corrections. Remember that quality is far more important than quantity.

Write your essays clearly and legibly in black or dark-blue ink. Cross out any errors you make.

Question 1

(Suggested time—40 minutes. This question counts as one-third of the total essay section score.)

In her poem "Siren Song," Margaret Atwood addresses the concern that women feel compelled to be alluring to attract a mate. Carefully read the poem. Then write an essay in which you analyze how poetic techniques such as imagery, irony, and allusion help to characterize the speaker's attitude toward the "Siren Song."

This is the one song everyone
would like to learn: the song
that is irresistible:

the song that forces men
to leap overboard in squadrons   5
even though they see the beached skulls

the song nobody knows
because anyone who has heard it
is dead, and the others can't remember.

Shall I tell you the secret   10
and if I do, will you get me
out of this bird suit?

I don't enjoy it here
squatting on this island
looking picturesque and mythical   15

with these two feathery maniacs,
I don't enjoy singing
this trio, fatal and valuable.

I will tell the secret to you,
to you, only to you.   20
Come closer. This song

is a cry for help: Help me!
Only you, only you can,
you are unique

at last. Alas   25
it is a boring song
but it works every time.

Question 2

(Suggested time—40 minutes. This question counts as one-third of the total essay section score.)

In this excerpt from Edith Wharton's "Roman Fever," the writer portrays two women meeting again in Rome after many years. Carefully read the passage. Then write an essay that describes how the author uses literary devices such as irony, diction, selection of details, and syntax to characterize the relationship between the two female protagonists.

Mrs. Slade drew her lids together in retrospect; and for a few moments the two ladies, who had been intimate since childhood, reflected how little they knew each other. Each one, of course, had a label ready to attach to the other's name; Mrs. Delphin Slade, for instance, would have told (5) herself, or anyone who asked her, that Mrs. Horace Ansley, twenty-five years ago, had been exquisitely lovely—no, you wouldn't believe it, would you? . . . though, of course, still charming, distinguished. . . . Well, as a girl she had been exquisite; far more beautiful than (10) her daughter Barbara, though certainly Babs, according to the new standards at any rate, was more effective—had more *edge*, as they say. Funny where she got it, with those two nullities as parents. Yes; Horace Ansley was—well, just the duplicate of his wife. Museum specimens of old (15) New York. Good-looking, irreproachable, exemplary. Mrs. Slade and Mrs. Ansley had lived opposite each other— actually as well as figuratively—for years. When the drawing-room curtains in No. 20 East 73rd Street were renewed, No. 23, across the way, was always aware of it. (20) And of all the movings, buyings, travels, anniversaries, illnesses—the tame chronicle of an estimable pair. Little of it escaped Mrs. Slade. But she had grown bored with it by the time her husband made his big *coup* in Wall Street, and when they bought in upper Park Avenue had already (25) begun to think: "I'd rather live opposite a speakeasy for a change; at least one might see it raided." The idea of seeing Grace raided was so amusing that (before the move) she launched it at a woman's lunch. It made a hit, and went the rounds—she sometimes wondered if it had (30) crossed the street, and reached Mrs. Ansley. She hoped not, but didn't much mind. Those were the days when respectability was at a discount, and it did the irreproachable no harm to laugh at them a little.

A few years later, and not many months apart, both (35) ladies lost their husbands. There was an appropriate exchange of wreaths and condolences, and a brief renewal of intimacy in the half-shadow of their mourning; and now, after another interval, they had run across each other in Rome, at the same hotel, each of them the modest (40) appendage of a salient daughter. The similarity of their lot had again drawn them together, lending itself to mild jokes, and the mutual confession that, if in old days it must have been tiring to "keep up" with daughters, it was now, at times, a little dull not to.

45

No doubt, Mrs. Slade reflected, she felt her unemployment more than poor Grace ever would. It was a big drop from being the wife of Delphin Slade to being his widow. She had always regarded herself (with a certain conjugal pride) as his equal in social gifts, as contributing her full share to the making of the exceptional couple they were: but the difference after his death was irremediable. As the wife of the famous corporation lawyer, always with an international case or two on hand, every day brought its exciting and unexpected obligation: the impromptu entertaining of eminent colleagues from abroad, the hurried dashes on legal business to London, Paris or Rome, where the entertaining was so handsomely reciprocated; the amusement of hearing in her wake: "What, that handsome woman with the good clothes and the eyes is Mrs. Slade—*the* Slade's wife? Really? Generally the wives of celebrities are such frumps."

50

55

60

Yes; being *the* Slade's widow was a dullish business after that. In living up to such a husband all her faculties had been engaged; now she had only her daughter to live up to, for the son who seemed to have inherited his father's gifts had died suddenly in boyhood. She had fought through that agony because her husband was there, to be helped and to help; now, after the father's death, the thought of the boy had become unbearable. There was nothing left but to mother her daughter; and dear Jenny was such a perfect daughter that she needed no excessive mothering. "Now with Babs Ansley I don't know that I *should* be so quiet," Mrs. Slade sometimes half-enviously reflected; but Jenny, who was younger than her brilliant friend, was that rare accident, an extremely pretty girl who somehow made youth and prettiness seem as safe as their absence. It was all perplexing—and to Mrs. Slade a little boring. She wished that Jenny would fall in love—with the wrong man, even; that she might have to be watched, out-maneuvered, rescued. And instead, it was Jenny who watched her mother, kept her out of drafts, made sure that she had taken her tonic. . . .

65

70

75

80

Mrs. Ansley was much less articulate than her friend, and her mental portrait of Mrs. Slade was slighter, and drawn with fainter touches. "Alida Slade's awfully brilliant; but not as brilliant as she thinks," would have summed it up; though she would have added, for the enlightenment of strangers, that Mrs. Slade had been an extremely dashing girl; much more so than her daughter, who was pretty, of course, and clever in a way, but had none of her mother's—well, "vividness," someone had once called it. Mrs. Ansley would take up current words

85

90

like this, and cite them in quotation marks, as unheard-of
audacities. No; Jenny was not like her mother. Sometimes   95
Mrs. Ansley thought Alida Slade was disappointed; on the
whole she had had a sad life. Full of failures and mistakes;
Mrs. Ansley had always been rather sorry for her. . . .

So these two ladies visualized each other, each
through the wrong end of her little telescope.   100

Question 3

(Suggested time—40 minutes. This question counts as one-third of the total essay section score.)

One of the most influential stages of maturation occurs when a child grapples with the authority of a father or father figure. Yet in some families the father is absent, either literally or figuratively. From the list below, choose a novel, play, or epic poem in which a character's relationship with a father or father figure, whether absent or present, plays a role in the meaning of the work as a whole. Be sure to address in your essay what kind of legacy or impact the father figure has on the protagonist.

Amadeus	*Oedipus Rex*
Ceremony	*Sister Carrie*
David Copperfield	*The Adventures of Huckleberry Finn*
Death of a Salesman	*The Aeneid*
Equus	*The Catcher in the Rye*
Fences	*The Glass Menagerie*
Great Expectations	*The Great Gatsby*
Hamlet	*The House on Mango Street*
Heart of Darkness	*The Scarlet Letter*
Master Harold and the Boys	*Their Eyes Were Watching God*
Native Son	*True West*

END OF EXAMINATION

ANSWERS FOR THE MULTIPLE-CHOICE QUESTIONS IN PRACTICE TEST 1

"BLACKBERRY EATING" BY GALWAY KINNELL

1. C	2. A	3. C	4. E	5. B
6. B	7. E	8. D	9. C	10. A
11. D	12. B	13. A		

"I GO BACK TO MAY 1937" BY SHARON OLDS

14. A	15. C	16. E	17. A	18. E
19. B	20. C	21. E	22. A	23. D
24. D	25. B	26. D		

"LET ME NOT TO THE MARRIAGE OF TRUE MINDS" BY WILLIAM SHAKESPEARE

27. C	28. A	29. D	30. B	31. A
32. C	33. A	34. B	35. D	36. C
37. D	38. C	39. C	40. B	41. D

EXCERPT FROM "A VERY OLD MAN WITH ENORMOUS WINGS" BY GABRIEL GARCÍA MARQUÉZ

42. A	43. D	44. C	45. B	46. D
47. E	48. E	49. A	50. D	51. A
52. C	53. D	54. C	55. E	

CALCULATING THE AP EXAM GRADE FOR PRACTICE TEST 1

Please keep in mind that these numbers are approximate. Two variables affect the computation every year: the number of multiple-choice questions and the difficulty levels of the essays. There is a slight curve created every year in terms of the numbers. However, remember that earning 15 points on the three essays combined and getting 55 percent right and marking as many as 11 wrong answers on the multiple-choice questions will generally produce a score of 3.

SCORING THE MULTIPLE-CHOICE SECTION

$$\underset{\text{number correct}}{\underline{\hspace{3cm}}} - (1/4 \times \underset{\text{number incorrect}}{\underline{\hspace{3cm}}}) = \underset{\text{multiple-choice score}}{\underline{\hspace{3cm}}}$$

SCORING THE FREE-RESPONSE SECTION

$$\underset{\substack{\text{Question 1} \\ \text{(0–9 score)}}}{\underline{\hspace{2cm}}} + \underset{\substack{\text{Question 2} \\ \text{(0–9 score)}}}{\underline{\hspace{2cm}}} + \underset{\substack{\text{Question 3} \\ \text{(0–9 score)}}}{\underline{\hspace{2cm}}} = \underset{\text{total essay score}}{\underline{\hspace{2cm}}}$$

COMPOSITE SCORE

$$1.23 \times \frac{\underline{\hspace{3cm}}}{\text{multiple-choice score}} = \frac{\underline{\hspace{3cm}}}{\substack{\text{weighted section I} \\ \text{score}}}$$

$$3.05 \times \frac{\underline{\hspace{3cm}}}{\text{free-response score}} = \frac{\underline{\hspace{3cm}}}{\substack{\text{weighted section II} \\ \text{score}}}$$

$$\frac{\underline{\hspace{2.5cm}}}{\substack{\text{weighted} \\ \text{section I}}} + \frac{\underline{\hspace{2.5cm}}}{\substack{\text{weighted} \\ \text{section II}}} = \frac{\underline{\hspace{2.5cm}}}{\text{composite score}}$$

DETERMINING THE AP EXAM GRADE

You now have a number between 0 and about 150. The composite scores are divided into five ranges, one for each AP grade. Each year that scale is adjusted. Generally, it goes like this:

Composite Score Range	AP Grade
112–150	5
95–110	4
76–94	3
50–75	2
0–49	1

PRACTICE TEST 2

AP ENGLISH LITERATURE AND COMPOSITION EXAMINATION
Section I: Multiple-Choice Questions
Number of questions: 55
Total time: 1 hour

Directions: This part consists of selections from prose works and questions on their content, form, and style. After reading each passage, choose the best answer to each question.

QUESTIONS 1–14. Carefully read "The Sick Rose" by William Blake before choosing your answers.

> O Rose, thou art sick!
> The invisible worm
> That flies in the night,
> In the howling storm,
>
> Has found out thy bed   5
> Of crimson joy,
> And his dark secret love
> Does thy life destroy.

1. Which of the following statements is correct?
   (A) The entire poem is grammatically classed as two paragraphs.
   (B) The entire poem is grammatically classed as an exclamation followed by a complex sentence.
   (C) The entire poem has the grammatical syntax of one simple sentence.
   (D) The entire poem defies grammatical dissection.
   (E) The entire poem lacks syntax.

2. Taken in its entirety, the poem
   (A) directly addresses the rose
   (B) uses the figure known as apostrophe
   (C) talks to a worm
   (D) both (A) and (B) are correct
   (E) both (B) and (C) are correct

3. The poem has which of the following rhyme schemes?
   (A) *abab*
   (B) *abcb*
   (C) *abcd*
   (D) *aabb*
   (E) *aaab*

4. The rose in the poem most likely refers to
   (A) the natural world's flower
   (B) the poetic world's symbol for love
   (C) the philosophical world's treatise on law
   (D) (A) and (B) only
   (E) (A) and (C) only

5. The "invisible worm" (line 2) may bring to mind
    (A) the positive image of a garden
    (B) a likeness of the biblical serpent
    (C) the image of penetrating wellness in the world
    (D) the image of wholeness in the world
    (E) the image of a lack of devastation

6. The word "invisible" (line 2) as it refers to the worm accentuates a marked symbol of
    (A) blithe devotion
    (B) filial closeness
    (C) corrupting stealth
    (D) benevolent satisfaction
    (E) awesome enthusiasm

7. The words "crimson joy" (line 6) may allude to
    (A) happy gratification
    (B) bewilderment
    (C) shame, embarrassment, and carnal gratification
    (D) fidelity and faithfulness
    (E) courtesy and civility

8. The grammatical subject of the verb "Has" in line 5 is
    (A) the worm
    (B) the flies
    (C) the joy
    (D) the rose
    (E) the storm

9. The pronoun "his" in line 7 has as its syntactical antecedent the word
    (A) joy
    (B) rose
    (C) storm
    (D) love
    (E) worm

10. The noun that is the subject of the verb "Does . . . destroy" (line 8) is
    (A) joy
    (B) worm
    (C) storm
    (D) love
    (E) rose

11. The ultimate meaning surrounding the rose must include
    (A) joy
    (B) bounty
    (C) righteousness
    (D) degeneration and decay
    (E) faith and hope

12. The words "life destroy" (line 8) are close to an example of
    (A) oxymoron
    (B) alliteration
    (C) euphony
    (D) caesura
    (E) elision

13. Lines 3–4, "That flies in the night, / In the howling storm," strongly suggest
    I. a vague yet irritating infestation
    II. a furtive event under cover of noise and darkness
    III. clandestine destruction
    (A) I only
    (B) I and II only
    (C) II and III only
    (D) I, II, and III
    (E) I and III only

14. The entire poem is classified as a(n)
    (A) epic
    (B) lyric
    (C) villanelle
    (D) enjambment
    (E) haiku

QUESTIONS 15–28. Carefully read the passage from the beginning of "Young Goodman Brown" by Nathaniel Hawthorne before choosing your answers.

Young Goodman Brown came forth at sunset into the street of Salem Village, but put his head back, after crossing the threshold, to exchange a parting kiss with his young wife. And Faith, as the wife was aptly named, thrust her own pretty head into the street, letting the wind play 5
with the pink ribbons of her cap while she called to Goodman Brown.

"Dearest heart," whispered she softly and rather sadly when her lips were close to his ear, "prithee, put off your journey until sunrise, and sleep in your own bed tonight. 10
A lone woman is troubled with such dreams and such thoughts that she's afeard of herself, sometimes. Pray, tarry with me this night, dear husband, of all nights in the year!"

"My love and my Faith," replied young Goodman 15
Brown, "of all nights in the year this one night must I tarry away from thee. My journey, as thou callest it, forth and back again must needs be done 'twixt now and sunrise. What, my sweet, pretty wife, dost thou doubt me already, and we but three months married!" 20

"Then God bless you!" said Faith with the pink ribbons, "and may you find all well when you come back."

"Amen!" cried Goodman Brown. "Say thy prayers, dear Faith, and go to bed at dusk, and no harm will come to thee." 25

So they parted; and the young man pursued his way until, being about to turn the corner by the meeting-house, he looked back and saw the head of Faith still peeping after him with a melancholy air in spite of her pink ribbons. 30

"Poor little Faith!" thought he, for his heart smote him. "What a wretch am I, to leave her on such an errand! She talks of dreams, too. Methought, as she spoke, there was trouble in her face, as if a dream had warned her what work is to be done tonight. But no, no! 'twould kill her to think it. Well; she's a blessed angel on earth and after this one night I'll cling to her skirts and follow her to Heaven." 35

With this excellent resolve for the future, Goodman Brown felt himself justified in making more haste on his present evil purpose. He had taken a dreary road, darkened by all the gloomiest trees of the forest, which barely stood aside to let the narrow path creep through, and closed immediately behind. It was all as lonely as could be; and there is this peculiarity in such a solitude, that the traveler knows not who may be concealed by the innumerable trunks and the thick boughs overhead so that with lonely footsteps he may be passing through an unseen multitude. 40 45

"There may be a devilish Indian behind every tree," said Goodman Brown to himself; and he glanced fearfully behind him as he added, "What if the devil himself should be at my very elbow!" 50

His head being turned back, he passed a crook of the road, and looking forward again beheld the figure of a man in grave and decent attire, seated at the foot of an old tree. He rose at Goodman Brown's approach and walked onward side by side with him. 55

"You are late, Goodman Brown," said he. "The clock of the Old South was striking as I came through Boston, and that is full fifteen minutes agone." 60

"Faith kept me back awhile," replied the young man with a tremor in his voice caused by the sudden appearance of his companion, though not wholly unexpected.

It was now deep dusk in the forest, and deepest in that part of it where these two were journeying. As nearly as could be discerned, the second traveler was about fifty years old, apparently in the same rank of life as Goodman Brown, and bearing a considerable resemblance to him, though perhaps more in expression than features. Still, they might have been taken for father and son. And yet, though the elder person was as simply clad as the younger, and as simple in manner too, he had an indescribable air of one who knew the world and would 65 70

not have felt abashed at the governor's dinner table or in   75
King William's court, were it possible that his affairs
should call him thither. But the only thing about him that
could be fixed upon as remarkable was his staff, which
bore the likeness of a great black snake, so curiously
wrought that it might almost be seen to twist and wriggle   80
itself like a living serpent. This, of course, must have been
an ocular deception, assisted by the uncertain light.

15. The word "prithee" (line 9) means
    (A) I love you
    (B) I have pride in you
    (C) I remember you
    (D) I pray thee
    (E) I feel nothing but revenge for you

16. The phrase "must needs" (line 18) has the modern meaning
    (A) I have secured it
    (B) I will not abide it
    (C) I cannot have it
    (D) I have an abundance
    (E) I am required to do it

17. The word "callest" (line 17) is the
    (A) archaic form of "to be callous"
    (B) archaic form of the past tense of "to call"
    (C) ancient word for "the unknown"
    (D) scientific measurement of temperature
    (E) religious term for "to convene"

18. The wife of Goodman Brown is
    (A) unnamed
    (B) known as Faith
    (C) known as Hope
    (D) called Mrs. Brown
    (E) called Goodwife or Goody Brown

19. The word "smote" (line 31) is
    (A) a verb meaning "to inflict a heavy blow"
    (B) a noun that is a synonym for the word "heart"
    (C) an adjective modifying the word "heart"
    (D) an article of clothing
    (E) a noun meaning tiny particle

20. "'There may be a devilish Indian behind every tree,' said Goodman
    Brown to himself; and he glanced fearfully behind him as he
    added, 'What if the Devil himself should be at my very elbow!'"
    (lines 51–52) shows all of the following EXCEPT
    (A) anxiety for the unknown
    (B) conjuring up false images
    (C) dread of the ambiguous
    (D) optimism in the face of danger
    (E) whistling past the graveyard

21. In line 75, the word "abashed" means all of the following EXCEPT
(A) contrite
(B) embarrassed
(C) ashamed
(D) assertive
(E) chagrined

22. Lines 36–37, "she's a blessed angel on earth and after this one night I'll cling to her skirts and follow her to Heaven," suggest that Goodman Brown thinks
(A) his wife will be his heavenly assurance and entree to paradise
(B) he will die before his wife
(C) his wife is really an angel of the Lord
(D) he will meet death alone
(E) he hates his wife

23. The words "had an indescribable air of one who knew the world," (lines 73–74) are a commentary on
(A) the clearness of the atmosphere
(B) the sagacious people in the world
(C) the song that they are about to sing
(D) the frightened townspeople
(E) the insight of timorous citizens

24. In line 53, the word "crook" is
(A) a noun meaning a long staff with one hook-shaped end
(B) a noun meaning a bend in the road
(C) a noun meaning someone who has committed a crime
(D) a verb meaning to bend or to cause to bend
(E) a noun meaning an entrance to a house

25. In line 80, the word "wrought" means all of the following EXCEPT
(A) put together
(B) created carefully
(C) shaped by hammering with tools
(D) purchased
(E) made delicately or elaborately

26. The phrase "like a living serpent"(line 81) is an example of
(A) onomatopoeia
(B) oxymoron
(C) lytotes
(D) metaphor
(E) simile

27. The phrase "which barely stood aside to let the narrow path creep through" (lines 41–42) is an example of
(A) reification
(B) personification
(C) alliteration
(D) oxymoron
(E) apostrophe

28. In the sentence "A lone woman is troubled with such dreams and such thoughts that she's afeard of herself, sometimes" (lines 11–12), the word "afeard" is
(A) a noun in apposition meaning "run"
(B) a verb in the present tense meaning "to be timorous"
(C) a verb in the present tense meaning "to be intimidated"
(D) a noun subject of the sentence meaning "hope"
(E) an adverb modifying "sometimes"

QUESTIONS 29–41. In this passage from *A Midsummer Night's Dream* (Act 5, Scene 1) by William Shakespeare, a speech prepared by Philostrate is read by Theseus. Carefully read the passage before choosing your answers.

THESEUS (*reads*). "The battle with the Centaurs, to be sung
By an Athenian eunuch to the harp"?
We'll none of that. That have I told my love,
In glory of my kinsman Hercules.
(*He reads.*) "The riot of the tipsy Bacchanals,   5
Tearing the Thracian singer in their rage"?
That is an old device; and it was played
When I from Thebes came last a conqueror.
(*He reads.*) "The thrice three Muses mourning for the death
Of Learning, late deceased in beggary"?   10
That is some satire, keen and critical,
Not sorting with a nuptial ceremony.
(*He reads.*) "A tedious brief scene of young Pyramus
And his love Thisbe; very tragical mirth"?
Merry and tragical? Tedious and brief?   15
That is, hot ice and wondrous strange snow.
How shall we find the concord of this discord?
PHILOSTRATE. A play there is, my lord, some ten words long,
Which is as brief as I have known a play.
But by ten words, my lord, it is too long,   20
Which makes it tedious. For in all the play
There is not one word apt, one player fitted.
And tragical, my noble lord, it is,
For Pyramus therein doth kill himself,
Which, when I saw rehearsed, I must confess,   25
Made mine eyes water; but more merry tears
The passion of loud laughter never shed.

29. The passage shows
(A) a critical commentary on four distinct choices of entertainment
(B) a criticism on one of three choices of entertainment
(C) a critical analysis on two choices of entertainment
(D) a positive analysis of two of three choices of entertainment
(E) a negative analysis of two of four choices of entertainment

30. The first of the evening's entertainment choices (lines 1–4) is sung by
(A) an Athenian relative of Cheiron
(B) a neutered vocalist
(C) a Greek dramatist
(D) Hercules himself
(E) a Greek poet

31. The evening's entertainment spoken about in lines 5–8 deals mainly
with a song about
(A) a morose event
(B) a Thracian frolic
(C) a flutist from Thrace
(D) a drunken singer who tears his clothes off
(E) a drunken party and brawl

32. The evening's distraction in lines 9–12 centers around
(A) three singers telling the story of the birth of the nine Muses
(B) a singer telling the story of mendicancy
(C) choristers depicting the story of the demise of education due to
insufficient funds
(D) choristers depicting the story of the nine Muses
(E) choristers telling the story of the happy death of learning

33. The diversion for the evening suggested in lines 13–17 centers
around
(A) a masterful monologue masquerading as comedy
(B) a full-length drama disguised as humor
(C) a serious interlude with deep political consequences
(D) a foolish playlet
(E) a trilogy

34. The lines "'very tragical mirth'? / Merry and tragical? Tedious and
brief? / That is, hot ice and wondrous strange snow. / How shall
we find the concord of this discord?" (14–17) offer several
examples of
(A) Freytag's pyramid
(B) oxymoron
(C) onomatopoeia
(D) metonymy
(E) synecdoche

35. Lines 18–22 show that the production spoken about is
(A) a great dramatic selection
(B) a great comic selection
(C) an example of great poetry
(D) no good because it is inordinately expensive
(E) no good because even though the actual play is brief, it is too
long

36. In line 22, the word "fitted" means
(A) restricted
(B) inappropriate
(C) unbefitting
(D) unacceptable
(E) prepared with proper equipment

37. The lines "That is some satire, keen and critical, / Not sorting with
a nuptial ceremony" (11–12) refer to
(A) the story of Pyramus and Thisbe
(B) the story told by the Muses
(C) the story from Thebes
(D) a song about Thisbe only
(E) a song about Pyramus only

38. "That is an old device" (line 7) means that
   (A) the story of Pyramus and Thisbe is an old one
   (B) the Muses' story is an old one
   (C) the story told with a harp is old
   (D) the Thracian singer uses an old-fashioned method
   (E) Theseus won't like it

39. "How shall we find the concord of this discord?" (line 17) is concerned with
   (A) fear and anxiety
   (B) love and hate
   (C) money and power
   (D) agreement and conflict
   (E) science and theater

40. "Made mine eyes water; but more merry tears / The passion of loud
laughter never shed" (lines 26–27) is a commentary on
   (A) the meager acting talent in the unsuitable interlude
   (B) the greatness of the work to be seen
   (C) the depth and acumen of those putting on the play
   (D) the depth of the play itself
   (E) the Muses' ability to sing

41. "Which, when I saw rehearsed, I must confess, /Made mine eyes water; but more merry tears" (lines 25–26) tells the audience that
   (A) lamentation and sorrow supplanted the tears of joy
   (B) laughter violently usurped the sadness
   (C) Pyramus killed Thisbe
   (D) Thisbe killed Pyramus
   (E) grief appropriated the laughter

QUESTIONS 42–55. Carefully read the following passage from "The Love Song of J. Alfred Prufrock" by T. S. Eliot before choosing your answers.

> Let us go then, you and I,
> When the evening is spread out against the sky
> Like a patient etherized upon a table;
> Let us go, through certain half-deserted streets,
> The muttering retreats   5
> Of restless nights in one-night cheap hotels
> And sawdust restaurants with oyster-shells:
> Streets that follow like a tedious argument
> Of insidious intent
> To lead you to an overwhelming question. . . .   10
> Oh, do not ask, "What is it?"
> Let us go and make our visit.
>
> In the room the women come and go
> Talking of Michelangelo.
>
> The yellow fog that rubs its back upon the window-panes,   15
> The yellow smoke that rubs its muzzle on the window-panes
> Licked its tongue into the corners of the evening,
> Lingered upon the pools that stand in drains,
> Let fall upon its back the soot that falls from chimneys,

Slipped by the terrace, made a sudden leap,   20
And seeing that it was a soft October night,
Curled once about the house, and fell asleep.

And indeed there will be time
For the yellow smoke that slides along the street,
Rubbing its back upon the window-panes;   25
There will be time, there will be time
To prepare a face to meet the faces that you meet;
There will be time to murder and create,
And time for all the works and days of hands
That lift and drop a question on your plate;   30
Time for you and time for me,
And time yet for a hundred indecisions,
And for a hundred visions and revisions,
Before the taking of a toast and tea.

In the room the women come and go   35
Talking of Michelangelo.

And indeed there will be time
To wonder, "Do I dare?" and, "Do I dare?"
Time to turn back and descend the stair,
With a bald spot in the middle of my hair—   40
(They will say: "How his hair is growing thin!")
My morning coat, my collar mounting firmly to the chin,
My necktie rich and modest, but asserted by a simple pin—
(They will say: "But how his arms and legs are thin!")
Do I dare   45
Disturb the universe?
In a minute there is time
For decisions and revisions which a minute will reverse.

For I have known them all already, known them all—
Have known the evenings, mornings, afternoons,   50
I have measured out my life with coffee spoons;
I know the voices dying with a dying fall
Beneath the music from a farther room.
    So how should I presume?

42. "I have measured out my life with coffee spoons" (line 51) refers to
    (A) living a contented life
    (B) living a life of joyous breakfasts
    (C) living life as an exhausted person would
    (D) living life with careful consideration and not without giving in
        to excitement or pleasure
    (E) living life without tea

43. In lines 37–38, "And indeed there will be time / To wonder, 'Do I
    dare?' and 'Do I dare?'" Prufrock is asking whether he should
    (A) have tea
    (B) make a declaration of love
    (C) have coffee
    (D) quit work
    (E) continue in his profession

44. "Like a patient etherized upon a table" (line 3) is a(n)
    (A) metaphor
    (B) apostrophe
    (C) oxymoron
    (D) simile
    (E) aubade

45. Lines 1–3 show evening as
    (A) lackadaisical
    (B) conflicted
    (C) idealistic
    (D) pedantic
    (E) deadly

46. Lines 8–9 are an example of
    (A) reification
    (B) personification
    (C) simile
    (D) lytotes
    (E) hyperbole

47. "In the room the women come and go / Talking of Michelangelo" (lines 35–36) is used as a refrain to express which of the following ideas?
    I.   Prufrock believes that if the women are interested in Michelangelo, they cannot be interested in him.
    II. Prufrock hates Michaelangelo.
    III. The women probably detest Prufrock.
    (A) I and II only
    (B) I only
    (C) II only
    (D) III and II only
    (E) III only

48. In "Let us go, through certain half-deserted streets, / The muttering retreats" (lines 4–5), the word "us" refers to
    (A) the poet and his alter-ego
    (B) the speaker and the listener
    (C) Prufrock and Eliot
    (D) God and man
    (E) business and industry

49. The title "The Love Song of J. Alfred Prufrock" is fitting for all of the following reasons EXCEPT
    (A) the poem deals with wanting to be loved
    (B) like most love songs, the poem has a refrain
    (C) the speaker is a lover even though he is a businessman
    (D) a love song is by definition a narrative poem
    (E) the poem focuses on romantic passion, which Prufrock feels has eluded him

50. "The muttering retreats / Of restless nights in one-night cheap hotels / And sawdust restaurants with oyster-shell" (lines 5–7) describes
    (A) times that, like the days, are also unsettled
    (B) great times on the noble side of life
    (C) times spent at the circus
    (D) bleak times spent in seedy places
    (E) times of silent religious retreat

51. In line 8, Eliot uses the word "streets" as
    (A) the question portion of a meticulous and uplifting contention
    (B) the question portion of an exhilarated and logical argument
    (C) the question portion of a monotonous and harmful argument
    (D) a rather charming and pretentious, yet stern, argument
    (E) nothing to do metaphorically with an argument

52. "To prepare a face to meet the faces that you meet" (line 27) suggests
    (A) artifice in day-to-day dealings
    (B) pride in enjoying life
    (C) humility in arguments
    (D) that love overcomes all deceit
    (E) veracity in meeting all challenges

53. Lines 43–44 show symbolically that the pin
    (A) represents a hatred for wearing simple tie pins
    (B) stands for all precious objects
    (C) shows that he longs to visit the land of Michelangelo
    (D) shows a contrast between his feigned appearance and his cowardice
    (E) stands for pilgrimage

54. In both line 41 and line 44, "They," in Prufrock's view, refers to people best described as
    (A) lackadaisical
    (B) manipulative
    (C) hopeful
    (D) benevolent
    (E) pernicious

55. The poem stresses an underlying sense of
    (A) poetic and literary success
    (B) romantic and passionate success
    (C) poetic and literary failure
    (D) dramatic and optimistic acceptance
    (E) personal and comacent triumph

STOP
END OF SECTION I

Section II: Essay Questions
Number of questions: 3
Reading time: 15 minutes
Writing time: 2 hours

Directions: Section II of this examination requires answers in essay form. The two hours are yours to divide among the three essay questions as you think best. To help you use your time well, the proctor may announce the time at which each question should be completed. If you finish any question before time is announced, you may go on to another question. You may go back at any time and work on any essay question you want.

Each essay will be judged on its clarity and effectiveness in dealing with the assigned topic and on the quality of the writing. In response to Question 3, select a work of recognized literary merit appropriate to the question. A good general rule is to use works of the same quality as those you studied in your Advanced Placement literature course(s).

After completing each question, you should check your essay for accuracy of punctuation, spelling, and diction; you are advised, however, not to attempt many longer corrections. Remember that quality is far more important than quantity.

Write your essays clearly and legibly in black or dark-blue ink. Cross out any errors you make.

Question 1

(Suggested time—40 minutes. This question counts as one-third of the total essay section score.)

In "The Value of Education" by Mark Halliday, the speaker gives his thoughts on that subject. Write an essay explaining how Halliday's use of figurative language, allusion, and tone conveys his indelicate and brash response to his subject and at the same time reveals much about the poet.

```
        I go now to the library. When I sit in the library
        I am not illegally dumping bags of kitchen garbage
        in the dumpster behind Clippinger Laboratory,
        and a very pissed-off worker at Facilities Management
        is not picking through my garbage and finding                5
        several yogurt-stained and tomato-sauce-stained envelopes
        with my name and address on them.
        When I sit in the library,
        I might doze off a little,
        and what I read might not penetrate my head               10
        which is mostly porridge in a bowl of bone.
        However, when I sit there trying to read
        I am not, you see, somewhere else being a hapless ass.
        I am not leaning on the refrigerator
        in the apartment of a young female colleague               15
        chatting with oily pep
        because I imagine she may suddenly decide to
        do sex with me while her boyfriend is on a trip.
        Instead I am in the library! Sitting still!
        No one in town is approaching my chair                     20
        with a summons, or a bill, or a huge fist.
        This is good. You may say,
        "But this is merely a negative definition of
        the value of education." Maybe so,
        but would you be able to say that                          25
        if you hadn't been to the library?
```

Question 2

(Suggested time—40 minutes. This question counts as one-third of the total essay section score.)

The following monologue comes at the end of *The Glass Menagerie,* by Tennessee Williams, which he referred to as "a memory play." In a well-organized essay describe how the author, using detail, diction, and syntax, makes memories elaborate and vivid. Show how the author makes a case for the importance of memories as distinct from reality.

TOM: I didn't go to the moon, I went much further—for
time is the longest distance between two places—
Not long after that I was fired for writing a poem on
the lid of a shoe-box. I left Saint Louis. I descended
the steps of this fire-escape for a last time and   5
followed, from then on, in my father's footsteps,
attempting to find in motion what was lost in
space—I traveled around a great deal. The cities
swept about me like dead leaves, leaves that were
brightly colored but torn away from the branches. I   10
would have stopped, but I was pursued by
something. It always came upon me unawares,
taking me altogether by surprise. Perhaps it was a
familiar bit of music. Perhaps it was only a piece of
transparent glass. Perhaps I am walking along a   15
street at night, in some strange city, before I have
found companions. I pass the lighted window of a
shop where perfume is sold. The window is filled
with pieces of colored glass, tiny transparent bottles
in delicate colors, like bits of a shattered rainbow.   20
Then all at once my sister touches my shoulder. I
turn around and look into her eyes . . . Oh, Laura,
Laura, I tried to leave you behind me, but I am more
faithful than I intended to be! I reach for a cigarette,
I cross the street, I run into the movies or a bar, I   25
buy a drink, I speak to the nearest stranger—
anything that can blow your candles out! . . . for
nowadays the world is lit by lightning! Blow out
your candles, Laura—and so good-bye . . .

Question 3

(Suggested time—40 minutes. This question counts as one-third of the total essay section score.)

Some say that the element in literature that really makes a good story is the conflict. This conflict must be a struggle between opposing forces. Most critics see conflict in four different and distinct ways:

- man versus man
- man versus nature
- man versus society
- man versus self

Many times characters react to the various conflicts in their lives in very different ways. Drawing on either a novel or play from the list below or another work of your choosing, write an essay describing how a character (it doesn't have to be the main character) experiences a conflict in at least two of the four areas, and show which is the more consequential of the conflicts you have chosen.

A Passage to India	*Othello*
All My Sons	*Pygmalion*
Death of a Salesman	*Return of the Native*
God's Favorite	*Rosencrantz and Guildenstern Are Dead*
Great Expectations	*Saint Joan*
Hamlet	*The Crucible*
Inherit the Wind	*The Grapes of Wrath*
Invisible Man	*The Importance of Being Earnest*
Jane Eyre	*The Jungle*
Lord of the Flies	*The Kite Runner*
Macbeth	*The Merchant of Venice*
Medea	*The Red Badge of Courage*
Murder in the Cathedral	*Their Eyes Were Watching God*
Native Son	*Things Fall Apart*
Oedipus Rex	*To Kill a Mockingbird*

END OF EXAMINATION

ANSWERS FOR THE MULTIPLE-CHOICE QUESTIONS IN PRACTICE TEST 2

"THE SICK ROSE" BY WILLIAM BLAKE

1. B	2. D	3. B	4. D	5. B
6. C	7. C	8. A	9. E	10. D
11. D	12. A	13. D	14. B	

EXCERPT FROM "YOUNG GOODMAN BROWN" BY NATHANIEL HAWTHORNE

15. D	16. E	17. B	18. B	19. A
20. D	21. D	22. A	23. B	24 B
25. D	26. E	27. B	28. B	

EXCERPT FROM A MIDSUMMER NIGHT'S DREAM BY WILLIAM SHAKESPEARE

29. A	30. B	31. E	32. C	33. D
34. B	35. E	36. E	37. B	38. D
39. D	40. A	41. B		

EXCERPT FROM "THE LOVE SONG OF J. ALFRED PRUFROCK" BY T. S. ELIOT

42. D	43. B	44. D	45. B	46. B
47. A	48. B	49. C	50. D	51. C
52. A	53. D	54. B	55. C	

Calculating the AP Exam Grade for Practice Test 2

Please keep in mind that these numbers are approximate. Two variables affect the computation every year: the number of multiple-choice questions and the difficulty levels of the essays. There is a slight curve created every year in terms of the numbers. However, remember that earning 15 points on the three essays combined and getting 55 percent right and marking as many as 11 wrong answers on the multiple-choice questions will generally produce a score of 3.

Scoring the Multiple-Choice Section

_____ — (1/4 x _____) = _____
number correct   number incorrect   multiple-choice score

Scoring the Free-Response Section

_____ + _____ + _____ = _____
Question 1   Question 2   Question 3   total essay score
(0–9 score)   (0–9 score)   (0–9 score)

Composite Score

1.23 x ——————————— = ———————————
       multiple-choice score   weighted section I
                                     score

3.05 x ——————————— = ———————————
       free-response score   weighted section II
                                     score

——————— + ——————— = ———————
weighted   weighted   composite score
section I   section II

Determining the AP Exam Grade

You now have a number between 0 and about 150. The composite scores are divided into five ranges, one for each AP grade. Each year that scale is adjusted. Generally, it goes like this:

Composite Score Range	AP Grade
112–150	5
95–110	4
76–94	3
50–75	2
0–49	1

Credits: p. 3, Shirley Jackson, "The Lottery" from THE LOTTERY AND OTHER STORIES. Copyright 1948, 1949 by Shirley Jackson. Copyright renewed © 1976, 1977 by Laurence Hyman, Barry Hyman, Mrs. Sarah Webster, and Mrs. Joanne Schnurer. Reprinted with the permission of Farrar, Straus & Giroux, LLC. p. 6, William Butler Yeats, "Sailing to Byzantium" from The Poems of W. B. Yeats: A New Edition, edited by Richard J. Finneran. Copyright 1928 by The Macmillan Company, renewed © 1956 by Georgie Yeats. Reprinted with the permission of Scribner, an imprint of Simon & Schuster Adult Publishing Group. All rights reserved. p. 9, Randall Jarrell, "The Death of the Ball Turret Gunner" from Complete Poems. Copyright © 1969 by Mary von Schrader Jarrell. Reprinted with the permission of Farrar, Straus & Giroux, LLC. p. 12, David Henry Hwang, "Trying to Find Chinatown." Reprinted with the permission of the author. p. 15, Imagine. Words and Music by John Lennon. Copyright © 1971 (Renewed 1999) LENONO MUSIC. All Rights Controlled and Administered by EMI BLACKWOOD MUSIC INC. All Rights Reserved. International Copyright Secured. Used by Permission. p. 18, Anne Sexton, "Cinderella" from TRANSFORMATIONS. Copyright © 1971 by Anne Sexton. Reprinted by permission of Houghton Mifflin Harcourt Publishing Company. All rights reserved. p. 26, Cathy Song, "Lost Sister" from PICTURE BRIDE. Copyright © 1983 by Cathy Song. Reprinted with the permission of Yale University Press. p. 30, Lawrence Ferlinghetti, "Christ Climbed Down" from A CONEY ISLAND OF THE MIND. Copyright © 1958 by Lawrence Ferlinghetti. Reprinted by permission of New Directions Publishing Corp. p. 35, William Shakespeare, "A Midsummer Night's Dream" from THE RIVERSIDE SHAKESPEARE, SECOND EDITION, edited by G. Blakemore Evans. Copyright © 1997 Heinle/Arts & Sciences, a part of Cengage Learning, Inc. Reprinted by permission, www.cengage.com/permissions p. 42, Sylvia Plath, "Daddy" from ARIEL. Copyright © 1961, 1963 by Ted Hughes. Reprinted by permission of HarperCollins Publishers and Faber and Faber, Ltd. p. 46, Archibald MacLeish, "Ars Poetica" from COLLECTED POEMS 1917-1982. Copyright 1926 by Archibald MacLeish. Copyright © 1985 by The Estate of Archibald MacLeish. Reprinted by permission of Houghton Mifflin Company. All rights reserved. p. 51, Arthur Miller, "Death of a Salesman." Copyright 1949, renewed © 1977 by Arthur Miller. Used by permission of Viking Penguin, a division of Penguin Group (USA) Inc. p. 56, Jimmy Santiago Baca, "Main Character" from Black Mesa Poems. Copyright © 1989 by Jimmy Santiago Baca. Reprinted with the permission of New Directions Publishing Corp. p. 59, Sophocles, "Oedipus Rex" from SOPHOCLES, THE OEDIPUS CYCLE: AN ENGLISH VERSION, translated by Dudley Fitts and Robert Fitzgerald. Copyright 1949 by Harcourt Brace & Company and renewed © 1977 by Cornelia Fitts and Robert Fitzgerald. Reprinted by permission of Harcourt, Inc. p. 62, Raymond Carver, "Cathedral" from CATHEDRAL. Copyright © 1983 by Raymond Carver. Used by permission of Alfred A. Knopf, a division of Random House, Inc. p. 70, Jorge Luis Borges, "The Plot" from THE ALEPH AND OTHER STORIES. Copyright © by Jorge Luis Borges. Used by permission of Penguin, a division of Penguin Group (USA) Inc. and The Wylie Agency, LLC. p. 75, Edward Albee, THE SANDBOX. Copyright © 1959 and renewed 1987 by Edward Albee. All rights reserved. CAUTION: Professionals and amateurs are hereby warned that "The Sandbox" is subject to a royalty. It is fully protected under the copyright laws of the United States of American and of all countries covered by the International Copyright Union (including the Dominion of Canada and the rest of the British Commonwealth), the Berne Convention, the Pan-American Copyright Convention and the Universal Copyright Convention as well as all countries with which the United States has reciprocal copyright relations. All rights, including professional/amateur state rights, motion picture, recitation, lecturing, public reading, radio broadcasting, television, video or sound recording, all other forms of mechanical or electronic reproduction, such as CD-ROM, CD-I, information storage and retrieval systems and photocopying, and the rights of translations in foreign languages, are strictly reserved. Particular emphasis is laid upon the matter of readings, permission for which must be secured from the author's agent in writing. Inquiries concerning rights should be addressed to: William Morris Agency, LLC, 1325 Avenue of the Americas, New

York, NY 10019, Attn: Eric Lupfer. p. 82, Dylan Thomas, "Do not go gentle into that good night" from THE POEMS OF DYLAN THOMAS. Copyright 1952 by Dylan Thomas. Reprinted with the permission of New Directions Publishing Corp. p. 85, Allen Ginsberg, "A Supermarket in California" from Collected Poems 1947-1980. Copyright © 1984 by Allen Ginsberg. Reprinted with the permission of HarperCollins Publishers. p. 94, Seamus Heaney, "Mid-Term Break" from OPENED GROUND: SELECTED POEMS 1966-1996. Copyright © 1998 by Seamus Heaney. Reprinted by permission of Farrar, Straus & Giroux, LLC and Faber & Faber, Ltd. p. 106, Donald Justice, "Men at Forty" from THE SUMMER ANNIVERSARIES. Copyright © 1967 by Donald Justice. Reprinted with the permission of Wesleyan University Press, www.wesleyan.edu/wespress. p. 117, Margaret Atwood, "Landcrab I" from Selected Poems II: Poems Selected and New 1976-1987. Copyright © 1987 by Margaret Atwood. Reprinted with the permission of Houghton Mifflin Company and Oxford University Press Canada. All rights reserved. p. 124, Sylvia Plath, "Spinster" from The Colossus and Other Poems. Copyright © 1962 by Sylvia Plath. Reprinted with the permission of Alfred A. Knopf, a division of Random House, Inc. and Faber and Faber, Ltd. p. 139, Langston Hughes, "Theme for English B" from The Collected Poems of Langston Hughes by Langston Hughes, coyright © 1994 by The Estate of Langston Hughes. Used by permission of Alfred A. Knopf, a division of Random House, Inc. p. 140, Billy Collins, "Introduction to Poetry" from THE APPLE THAT ASTONISHED PARIS. Copyright © 1988 by Billy Collins. Reprinted with the permission of the University of Arkansas Press. p. 143, Elizabeth Bishop, "The Fish" from THE COMPLETE POEMS 1927-1979. Copyright © 1979, 1983 by Alice Helen Methfessel. Reprinted by permission of Farrar, Straus & Giroux, LLC. p. 151, D. C. Berry, "On Reading Poems to a Senior Class at South High" from DIVORCE BOXING. Reprinted with the permission of Eastern Washington University Press. p. 154, Joyce Carol Oates, "Where Are You Going, Where Have You Been?" from WHERE ARE YOU GOING, WHERE HAVE YOU BEEN?: SELECTED EARLY STORIES. Copyright © 1993 by The Ontario Review, Inc. Reprinted with the permission of John Hawkins & Associates, New York. p. 158, John Updike, "A&P" from PIGEON FEATHERS AND OTHER STORIES. Copyright © 1962, and renewed 1990 by John Updike. Used by permission of Alfred A. Knopf, a division of Random House, Inc. p. 161, Henrik Ibsen, "A Doll House" from THE COMPLETE MAJOR PROSE PLAYS OF HENRIK IBSEN, translated by Rolf Fjelde. Copyright © 1965, 1970, 1978 by Rolf Fjelde. Used by permission of Dutton Signet, a division of Penguin Group (USA) Inc. p. 164, Dave Eggers, "Accident" from THE GUARDIAN (April 16, 2005). Copyright © 2005 by Dave Eggers. Reprinted with the permission of the author. p. 177, Galway Kinnell, "Blackberry Eating" from MORTAL ACTS, MORTAL WORDS. Copyright © 1980 by Galway Kinnell. Reprinted by permission of Houghton Mifflin Harcourt Publishing Company. All rights reserved. p. 179, Sharon Olds, "I Go Back to May 1937" from THE COLD CELL. Copyright © 1987 by Sharon Olds. Used by permission of Alfred A. Knopf, a division of Random House, Inc. p. 184, Gabriel García Márquez, "A Very Old Man with Enormous Wings" from LEAF STORM AND OTHER STORIES. Copyright © 1971 by Gabriel García Márquez. Reprinted by permission of HarperCollins Publishers. p. 190, Margaret Atwood, "Siren song" from SELECTED POEMS 1965-1975. Copyright © 1976 by Margaret Atwood. Reprinted by permission of Houghton Mifflin Company and Oxford University Press Canada. All rights reserved. p. 191, Edith Wharton, "Roman Fever" from ROMAN FEVER AND OTHER STORIES. Copyright 1934 by Liberty Magazine. Copyright renewed © 1962 by William R. Tyler. Reprinted with permission of Scribner, a division of Simon & Schuster Adult Publishing. p. 205, T. S. Eliot, "The Love Song of J. Alfred Prufrock" from T. S. ELIOT: THE COMPLETE POEMS AND PLAYS 1909-1950. Reprinted with the permission of Faber & Faber, Ltd. p. 210. Mark Halliday, "The Value of Education" from SLATE (June 21, 2000). Reprinted with the permission of the author. p. 211, Tennessee Williams, THE GLASS MENAGERIE. Copyright 1945 by The University of the South, renewed © 1973 by Tennessee Williams. Reprinted by permission of Georges Borchardt, Inc. on behalf of the Tennessee Williams Estate.